I FILL THIS
SMALL SPACE

❊

D1568180

I FILL THIS SMALL SPACE

The Writings of a Deaf Activist

Lawrence R. Newman

David J. Kurs, Editor

Gallaudet University Press
Washington, DC

Gallaudet University Press
Washington, DC 20002
http://gupress.gallaudet.edu

Library of Congress Cataloging-in-Publication Data
Newman, Lawrence R., 1925–
I fill this small space : the writings of a deaf activist / Lawrence R. Newman ; David J.
Kurs, editor.
p. cm.
ISBN 978-1-56368-408-1 (alk. paper)
1. Deaf—Education—United States. 2. Deaf—United States—Means of communication.
3. Deaf—United States—Social conditions. I. Kurs, David J. II. Title.
HV2430.N39 2009
362.4'2—dc22

2009012622

⊗ The paper used in this publication meets the minimum requirements of American
National Standard for Information Sciences—Permanence of Paper for Printed Library
Materials, ANSI Z39.48-1984.

To Betty
My Wife, My Angel

Contents

Part One: On Deaf Education

On the Least Restrictive Environment

On Teaching Standards and Certification

On Bilingual Education

Part Four: On a Mixed Bag — Columns and Poetry on (a) Deaf Life

Columns

Poems

Part Five: On the Light Side—Humorous Approaches to Deaf Education and Experience

Acknowledgments

Thanks to

My brother Leonard, who took me to libraries, could fingerspell and interpret.

Bernard Bragg, whose continuing support and push led to the publication of this book.

To the following, who gave me helpful suggestions during my early writing years:

Dr. Richard Brill
Dr. McCay Vernon
Dr. Robert Lennan
Merv Garretson.

And to DJ Kurs, especially, whose labors and editing have compacted a lifetime of writings into this book.

The Ballet of the Hands

Observe:
How fingers curl and paint
Until out of airy nothingness
Words and pictures leap and dance
With wondrous grace and beauty of design—
The ballet of the hands.

Reflect:
An open door, a ray of light,
A history of struggle to survive
The choking confines of man's mind
Until thrives in home and meeting place
Hands that sculpt, talk and sing—
Our very own. O palpable air.

Think:
Motionless or fluid, curled or uncurled
One finger, one flick of the wrist,
One sweep of the hands speak volumes,
Evoke happiness or grief, stir minds
As if by some magic alchemy.
O for such a gift raise your eyes and praise.

Study:
The face complementary, alive,
Vibrant the body, coiled or uncoiled
In mute chorus to the dancing hands
All converging in three dimensional grace.
O communication sure and joyous.

See:
The ballet of the hands,
How they portray
A falling leaf with a feathery touch
The force and power of Thor's thunder,
The parade of history in one hour,
The soft beauty of confessed love,
The word of God . . . O let us all arise
And in chorus sing a tableau of praise.

The Odyssey of a Deaf Activist

An Introduction

LAWRENCE NEWMAN

It was the late 1960s. The "Little Paper Family"—newsletters sent out by state schools for the deaf—had initiated a prolific exchange in print of ideas, thoughts, and opinions. Earlier, *The Cavalier* and *The Spectrum* had been among the first nationwide publications of, by, and for the deaf; then came *The Silent Worker*, which would become *The Deaf American*. At the time, these publications were the only national platform deaf people had to voice their thoughts and feelings, in contrast to the plethora of newsletters, magazines, blogs, and web sites that come from deaf people today. American Sign Language (ASL) lay hidden in the closet during these days, as the oral philosophy dominated the majority of schools and programs for the deaf, as most parents of deaf children were hostile to the use of the hands for communicating purposes, as deaf representatives on boards and organizations serving deaf people were a rarity, as deaf administrators of schools and programs for the deaf were almost unheard of. It was a time before a more enlightened parent organization—the International Association of Parents of the Deaf (IAPD), now called the American Society of Deaf Children (ASDC), was established, before the Americans with Disabilities Act (ADA) came into existence, before built-in captioned television sets were required by law.

It was at this time that I felt there was extremism among the proponents of the oral philosophy, that parents did not have a balanced view of what was involved and what mattered in the education of their deaf children. It should be understood that the articles and speeches collected here appeared at a time when the atmosphere was hostile to the use of sign language, when there was rampant paternalism, and before the Deaf President Now (DPN) movement that electrified not only deaf people but the whole world. It was a time when we were somewhat acquiescent, somewhat milquetoasty.

It was a time of heightened oral-manual controversies, of threats to balanced educational approaches. I seemed to have been a lonely figure at that time and the words and the style may be different and the write-ups less sophisticated but the goal was always to awaken the conscience and enlighten the minds of those in our world as well as many who were on the fringes, if not outside, of our lives.

Today's deaf writers appear in force, writing on a broad range of topics with aplomb, candidness, and a high measure of skill about their experiences of what it is like to be deaf. Deaf people have every right to be proud of them. They should be offered our praise and support. I can only hope that this collection of published writings can be of some

Larry at work as assistant superintendent of the Riverside School for the Deaf, California.

historical significance to these writers, their readers, and to anyone that comes across the deaf world.

It is gratifying to note that we are in a more enlightened time compared to the time when there were none so deaf as those who would not listen. More and more parents of deaf children are becoming sophisticated and aware of different perspectives and approaches in education and the development of the whole deaf child. A veritable cornucopia of linguists, scholars, and researchers have emerged out of the woods and shown us the complexity inherent in the field of deafness and the indispensable role sign language plays in the well-being of a large number of deaf people. As we come to understand the priorities and values in educating the deaf child, extremism in thinking of methods of communication or approaches seems to be fading. However, there are some unknowns on the horizon. What impacts will cochlear implants and other rapidly advancing technologies have on deaf culture, in fact, on deafness itself? Will generations yet unborn come to look upon us as antediluvian and relegate us into the dustbin of history?

Or will we still be, in the words of Harry Best, "The most misunderstood among the sons of men but the gamest of them all," somehow still surviving?[1]

---

1. Harry Best, *Deafness and the Deaf in the United States* (New York: Macmillan, 1943).

From the Small Space

A Biography of Lawrence Newman

DAVID J. KURS

In 1968, the John Tracy Clinic, a prominent oral education academy in Los Angeles, published a widely disseminated pamphlet that addressed parents of deaf children with the title: "Talk, Talk, Talk, Talk." The materials encouraged parents to continue talking because one day their child would eventually catch on. Lawrence Newman, at the time a math teacher at the California School for the Deaf, Riverside, and a father of four, fired back with an allegorical story in *The Deaf American* with the title "See, See, See, See!" that portrayed a blind student who was admonished to see by his parents and teachers. Two years later in the same magazine, he fired back at the same institution: "the minds of all civilized people are reached by communication in one form or another. When one of the five senses is no longer functioning, substitutes are sought to fill the void. The deaf themselves have found that manual communication is the greatest substitute available."

Dr. Edgar L. Lowell, the administrator of the John Tracy Clinic, wrote back in response:

> I would much prefer to have my child taught by a good manual teacher like Newman, "California's Teacher of the Year," than I would by some of the poor oral teachers that I have observed. . . . All parents, whether their children are hearing or deaf, are in for a good deal of frustration and disappointment . . . I just want to put down the notion that the oral method is to blame for all the disappointments and frustrations of the parents of deaf children. (see pp. 96–97, this volume)

In response, Newman thanked him and then said, "the fact that all parents experience frustration is no defense for adding to the frustration one hundredfold" (see p. 100, this volume).

The cultural battles that were fought in the 1960s and 1970s between the old guard of administrators of schools for the deaf and a nascent class of deaf educators would come to influence trends in deaf education for the rest of the century. Deaf teachers like Newman bristled at the absence of deaf school administrators and the continuing dominance of oral education, which they had undergone as children and which they felt was destined to fail.

Newman remained a loyal soldier, forging ahead in this battleground, by persistently highlighting his experiences as an educator and parent in publications such as *The Deaf American*. His success as a teacher and pundit would eventually propel him toward administrative positions, towards a role as an in-demand speaker logging hundreds of thousands of miles, and towards the presidency of the National Association of the Deaf (NAD). After his retirement in 1988, Newman has remained active in the community and continues to wax eloquently on the shifting landscapes of deaf education.

Astute observers will credit Newman's spirit and the need to correct the wrongs of the world to his upbringing by immigrant parents. Born on March 23, 1925, he was the third son of Isaac and Toby Newman (his older brothers George and Leonard were eleven and five years old, respectively.) The couple had met in their shared apartment in New York City—Toby's sister had married Isaac's brother—after they had emigrated from Poland. Isaac worked as a baker, a trade he had learned as an apprentice to his uncles in the old country, and eventually came to own the Garden Bake Shop, a small bakery that catered to the neighborhood. Their marriage lasted seventy-six years.

Mischievous and scampish, Newman possessed a generous streak. On a visit to her parents in Poland in 1932, Toby gave her son a box of chocolates to alleviate the dullness of the transatlantic journey. Newman, preferring to share, gave away the chocolates to other children. When he was six, he gave a ride-on fire truck, a cherished present from an aunt, to a neighborhood boy who did not have any toys.

At the age of five, Newman contracted mastoiditis, the result of chronic ear infection. The doctor, while performing myringotomy, a procedure intended to relieve swelling within the ear, cut the seventh cranial nerve that traversed Newman's middle ear. The accidental incision resulted in left facial nerve palsy and made Newman deaf: "I remember the ether administered like a suction cup on my face and my body floating back and forth, and waking up from nothingness, swathed in bandages. I saw

Larry's parents, December 1982.

my father at the foot of my bed fighting to hold back tears. He knew I would never hear again, but I did not realize it for a long time."

A sickly child, Newman spent much of his time in hospitals until the age of seven. He battled ailments such as pneumonia and scarlet fever. He later wrote about a visit to the hospital:

An ambulance came and paramedics carried me out of the building on a stretcher. I peeked through the sheet that covered me and saw rows of people lined up, watching me being carried to the ambulance. Inside, the paramedic was flirting with the nurse—what an ironic scenario. I was sick and there was the paramedic and the young nurse laughing.

In the hospital, there was a boy with a pockmarked face in a bed that was partitioned by a glass enclosure. All of a sudden, he went berserk and started to scratch his face, opening the scabs and blood came flowing out. I screamed to notify the nurses, and they came to restrain him. Across the room, there was a fastidious teenaged girl who did everything neatly and precisely: she folded her napkins during mealtime, cut the meat carefully and chewed slowly, and arranged her tissue paper into neat stacks. When I read *The Canterbury Tales* in college, there she was: the Prioress who was perfect in every way and neat in every activity.

Without knowing it, Newman was undergoing the process that so many deafened people undergo: filling up the void left by the loss of sound with visual processing. "The visual replaced the auditory. My eyes darted everywhere, seeking answers to puzzling questions festering in my mind. As I understood visual things, they left an impact on my mind. If I did something neatly, it was because of that teenage girl in the hospital across from my bed."

The boy was also confronted with an affliction that accompanies the onset of deafness for many: bouts of frustration and rebellion. He wrote on the walls of his family's apartment, begging his parents to "leave the place that made me deaf." After being refused a slice of a three-tier wedding cake that his father had just baked, he sat on the cake. Toby and Isaac chose not to discipline their son, instead blaming the doctor that operated on him.

Newman threw another monumental tantrum in 1932: Toby had taken him to the Lexington School for the Deaf in New York City for the first time. The white uniform of the dietician, the dormitory beds laid out in a row, and the white walls were too close to the experience of the loathed hospital for the boy. His mother whisked him away from the building, and it took months before he agreed to go to classes regularly.

Lexington taught using the oral method, and sign language was forbidden. If a student was caught signing, the entire class was forced to stand up, hold their arms up, and close their eyes for five minutes. The instructors relished the carte blanche they held over the students—when a boy drew a man with a purple crayon, the teacher screamed at him: "Did you ever see a purple man, a purple man?"

For his first years at the school, Newman chattered away in the classroom, in the hallways, and at every possible moment. "You remind me of a chicken strutting around with its head cut off, speaking to everyone as if you could still hear," a dormitory counselor told him.

When Lexington became an all-girls school, Newman transferred to the New York School for the Deaf, better known as Fanwood, in White Plains, NY. Newman picked up sign language at the military school; with this came the usual accelerated period of educational development. At one time, Newman roomed with Bernard Bragg, who would go on to become a noted deaf performer and a lifelong friend. Bragg remembers, "I was five and I watched Larry pray by the window every night. His hands were clasped and his lips kept moving. I wondered what he was praying for."

During weekends home from school, the boy would read all day long in bed. "When I got out of bed, my legs would collapse from numbness and I would fall to the ground." Toby felt the boy should lead a normal life and dutifully took him to other children's birthday parties. At a party, each child sang a favorite song; when it was Newman's turn, he simply screamed, "Awwwrrrrhhhhh!" and stopped only when the children and adults clapped.

The protective Toby forbade Newman from crossing the street without calling "Mom!" from the street. At her son's call, Toby would pop her head out of the apartment window and give him the okay to go ahead and cross the street. They did not have to worry about infuriating the others in the building—everyone knew the deaf boy's voice.

In high school, Toby and Isaac hired an algebra tutor for their son because four out of six hours of class time were dedicated to learning the vocation of printing. Newman was the editor of the school newsletter, *Fanwood Flashes,* and played tackle on the football team despite weighing only 135 pounds and having trouble breathing. The other players pounded on him during practice, but he earned their respect by calling the plays during games.

Newman's brother Lenny, a deputy district attorney, learned how to fingerspell and took his younger brother to libraries. When Newman was sixteen, Lenny gave him his district attorney's badge so that he could get past the policemen who were serving as security at the Polo Grounds for the Joe Louis–Billy Conn boxing match. Lenny passed on his interest in politics to Newman, and told him that if girls avoided him because of his paralyzed face, to ignore them because they couldn't see him for what he was.

The valedictorian of his graduating class, Newman went to Gallaudet College in the summer of 1943. His real education began there—not only from the deaf professors, but also from kindred souls in the residence halls. He quickly befriended Merv Garretson of Wyoming, who would later go on to become a renowned school administrator and deaf leader, over their shared love for literature and poetry. Newman shared the packages of baked goods shipped in from Isaac with his classmates. When Isaac visited the campus for the first time, Newman took him to

Brother Leonard with their father.

a soda fountain across the street. Shocked that all the students at the counter were deaf, Isaac paid the tab for everyone.

Newman assumed leadership positions in various organizations on campus and became the number two at his fraternity, Kappa Gamma. Newman manifested his deep love for sports: he ran the six-mile for the cross country team and the 880-meter for the track team, but it took him two hours to recover from each race. He later learned that he was short of breath because he could only breathe through one nostril. In his senior year, he began going out with Betty Mae Hartmann, who later became his wife. Their marriage has come to last more than fifty-seven years.

After graduating in 1948, at the encouragement of Dr. Powrie Vaux Doctor, who had suggested the nuns there would be helpful, Newman enrolled at the Catholic University of America in Washington, D.C., in the days before interpreting was a standard practice. On the first day of class, one of his professors announced, "If you believe in God, you will help that deaf man." After every class, the nuns gave the deaf man handwritten transcripts of lectures and discussions. If the professor said, "Good morning," the nuns would write it down. Graduating in 1950 with a master's

Larry and Betty at their fiftieth wedding anniversary.

degree in English Literature, Newman had considered pursuing a doctorate but decided not to when he realized he would have to master Latin and
German on top of French, which he had already passed.

Putting on hold his dream of becoming a writer, Newman took a
teaching post in upstate New York at the Central New York School for
the Deaf, in Rome. Thinking he would teach English, he arrived on
campus to find out the school had assigned him a schedule full of math
classes. On weekends, Newman wrestled with the math problems that
he would teach that week; later, he would attribute his teaching ability
to this experience of learning along with the students.

On the Rome campus, Newman met and befriended Robert Green-mun, the secretary/treasurer of NAD. A wit and a skilled writer, Greenmun was known for his columns in *The Deaf American* that mocked the misconceptions hearing people had of deaf people. Greenmun wrote letters late into the night, and his practice made an impression on Newman. In response to a reader who asked, "Do the deaf swim?" Greenmun wrote back in response, "In order to swim I suppose we must paddle with our ears." Newman was moved by Greenmun to start writing for the magazine, telling others that he did it "for a cause, for the rights of deaf people."

Through Greenmun, Newman was exposed to a crowd of erudite, postlingually deaf leaders who were known for their signing and oratory skills: Byron B. Burnes, the venerable president of NAD, NAD vice president Larry Yolles, and the legendary fundraiser David Peikoff. They eagerly mentored their young protégé, whose understanding, knowledge, and leadership qualities blossomed with each point of interaction. Newman later wrote how Greenmun engaged the young man "with discussions of the many forms of discrimination the deaf faced, the lack of access, the many injustices, the paternalistic attitudes, and how NAD's hands were tied due to the lack of funds." He traveled with Peikoff and Burnes as they traveled across the country, giving speeches. He saw the importance of fighting for deaf rights and listened as an older generation explained how they had fought for the right to drive.

The move to Riverside, California, to teach at the new California School for the Deaf (CSDR) in 1953 precipitated a cutback in activism as Newman shifted his energies to dedicated instruction. Newman had hoped that he would be able to teach English, but again, the only position open was for a math teacher. "It was my worst subject, but I ended up teaching it for twenty years." He was motivated by the success of his students. A famously exacting teacher, he kept his students late in class and even barged in another classroom when his students did not show up on time. If his students were unable to answer the two questions posted at the beginning of each class, he knew that they had not done their homework and they had to come back after school had ended for the day. Many of his students went on to achieve twelfth-grade-level competency on the Stanford Achievement Test in math. In a nationwide math survey of deaf schools and programs, his students placed first in computation and fourth in problem solving.

The 1950s and 1960s witnessed an influx of deaf teachers into the residential schools for the deaf. The deaf teachers knew that they were hired to provide support and friendship to the students, and that hearing teachers were expected to do the heavy lifting in terms of instruction. After regular visits to Newman's classroom, the august founding superintendent of CSDR, Dr. Richard Brill, nominated Newman for the California Teacher of the Year Award in 1968.

Newman beat out thousands of candidates for the award. "It is rather remarkable for a deaf person to receive a master's degree in English, but Mr. Newman was able to qualify for this. Later he changed his area of interest and has done extensive graduate work in mathematics. Mr. Newman's contributions to his students and to his profession have certainly earned him the title, California's Teacher of the Year," State Superintendent of Public Instruction Max Rafferty said when presenting Newman with the award. "The impact of my selection can easily be underestimated where educational services for the deaf are involved," Newman says in retrospect. "It was a landmark in my career. Doors opened." Newman received bags of letters from a public who was astounded that there was such a thing as a deaf teacher. One ten-year-old girl wrote to Newman, "How can you teach when my teacher who can hear cannot teach?"

An administrative position, heretofore thought unattainable, was within sight. Newman received a master's in administration from California State University Fullerton and became a master teacher, training teachers at the deaf education program at the California State University, Los Angeles.

Almost on cue, Newman was thrust into another role: that of a parent of a deaf child, when his youngest, Carol Lee, was born in 1969. He and Betty tackled their new role with vigor: Newman chronicled Carol's language development in a journal, which eventually became the article "Cherry Blossoms Come to Bloom" (see p. 122, this volume). The experience prompted Newman to write articles on language acquisition through word-meaning association, the modeling of the English language, the development of writing and reading skills, and the loss of language that occurs when a language foundation is absent. To this day,

Newman strongly advocates the methods of word-meaning association and modeling of the English language to deaf students.

Newman became the second president of the International Association of Parents of the Deaf (today the American Society for Deaf Children), and was a vocal participant at the meeting which led to the founding of the Independently Merging Parent Associations of California Together for the Hearing-Impaired (IMPACT-HI), which has battled the Least Restrictive Environment (LRE) movement's threat to state residential schools and continues to be an influential organization of parents of deaf children (see pp. 23–39, this volume).

Dr. Ursula Bellugi, the famed linguist from the Salk Institute in La Jolla, California, selected Carol as a subject for a long-term study of language acquisition. For the first five years of Carol's life, Bellugi and her research assistants tracked Carol's development during weekends. Bellugi's studies came to prove Newman's strong belief that children with strong foundations in sign language acquire strong foundations in English.

Newman's activism renewed during this period: he served on various boards (including the NAD Board), became the vice president of the California Association of the Deaf, and traveled to give speeches.

Larry and Betty with their children. From left to right, Warner, Rochelle, son-in-law Sandy, Lauren, Carol.

He began publishing articles in *The Deaf American* written with a drollness that matched that of the *Los Angeles Times* columnist Jack Smith. He wrote book reviews and articles about math instruction in the *American Annals of the Deaf,* and developed the booklet "Visual Aids in Mathematics" for the California Department of Education. His literary career hit new heights when his poem "Girl with a Whirligig" appeared in the nationwide journal *Social Education* (see p. 131, this volume).

The oral method of instruction received the brunt of Newman's activist columns. He remembers, "The Central Institute for the Deaf, which was the premier stronghold of oralism along with the Clarke School [in Massachusetts], distributed a poster of Koko, the signing ape, with the caption: 'Do you want your child to be like the ape and sign?' The Alexander Graham Bell Association [a strong advocate for oralism] sent a letter of protest to NBC when they featured signing members of the National Theatre of the Deaf." Newman spoke in favor of the flexible approaches of Simultaneous Communication and Total Communication[2] in front of hostile parents who were determined to normalize their deaf children through rigorous speech and lipreading instruction. "At one of my talks, an oralist administrator blew up and disrupted my talk while foaming at the mouth. He eventually gave up, walking and screaming down the aisle. I remember feeling relief that I didn't have to listen to them vilify sign language anymore."

Fearful that parents would transfer their children out of the school if there were deaf teachers at the preschool, primary, or elementary levels—or even deaf administrators at any level—schools and programs for the deaf were reluctant to make changes to accommodate the ever-growing contingent of deaf teachers. In 1974, when there were hardly any deaf administrators, Newman was selected to become the principal of the Taft School for the Aurally Handicapped in Santa Ana, California. He promptly brought five deaf teachers into the elementary department. He credited the Teacher of the Year Award for providing him with administrative free rein: "These times are a far cry from what we see

---

2. Simultaneous Communication is also known as SimCom. Total Communication is a whole learning model developed by Roy Holcomb. Today, this is often confused with SimCom; however, it encourages the appropriate communication method suited for the child's need.

today: numerous deaf administrators and deaf preschool- and elementary-level teachers." At Taft, Newman received gratitude from parents who had transferred their children from the John Tracy Clinic—their communication at home had changed dramatically with the introduction of sign language into the household.

Armed with the administrative experience he had gained at Taft, Newman went back to CSDR in 1977 as the assistant superintendent. He initiated a staff evaluation process emphasizing classroom visits by the principal and developed a lesson plan design format based on the time spent on tasks. He oversaw the construction of an educational life skills project promoting hands on learning called "Team Village": a mini-village composed of stores, a post office, a TTY communication setup, and so on.

Newman's alma mater, Gallaudet College, recognized his achievements by awarding him an honorary doctorate in 1978. For Newman, the experience was bittersweet: "As I received the doctoral regalia, I looked into the crowd and saw my father cry. I was reminded of the last time I saw him cry: at the foot of my hospital bed after I lost my hearing, where I laid swathed in bandages."

After leading an impromptu fundraising campaign at the 1984 NAD Convention in Salt Lake City that netted $35,000, Newman ran and captured the NAD presidency in 1986, benefiting from the fame he had gained when he was named California's Teacher of the Year and persistent campaigning by his good friend Bernard Bragg at the convention. Heading a murderer's row of renowned board members including Dr. Lawrence Stewart, Dr. Harvey Corson, Dr. Roz Rosen, and Philip Bravin, he dedicated his presidency to the struggle in favor of appropriate education policies by forming a task force on PL 94–142 (now called IDEA) and initiating the National Committee on Equal Educational Opportunities for Deaf Children (NCEEOD). He argued passionately against the concept of Least Restrictive Environment before the Commission on the Education of the Deaf (COED) and met with the powerful Schools Are For Everyone (SAFE) lobby to counteract opposition to residential schools (the education community saw them as segregated facilities).

"It was a turbulent period for the education of the deaf," remembers Newman. A powerful organization, The Association of the Severely Handicapped (TASH), counting Assistant Secretary of Education

Madeline Will among its allies, waged a battle against segregated schools. Will's definition of LRE, which called for educating deaf children in hearing schools, threatened the existence of residential schools of the deaf. Newman and the NAD Board also campaigned to ease laws that made it difficult for teachers of the deaf to acquire state certification and passed a Deaf Child's Bill of Rights with the governing adage: "What is appropriate for the child comes first. There should be various options to meet that option." He was influential in prompting the California Department of Education to distribute a brochure with an illustration showing various programs radiating out from a deaf child in the center of a diagram. "Thanks to this struggle, residential schools continued to thrive with some exceptions; namely, the dark cloud of cochlear implants professing to normalize deaf and hard of hearing children," Newman later wrote.

In 1990, the Americans with Disabilities Act (ADA) was signed into law during his second term. Newman marched with Gallaudet students to the Capitol during the Deaf President Now protest in favor of a deaf president for the university in March 1988, led a nationwide protest in demand of more closed captioning, and marched at CBS Studios to get the television show *Dallas* captioned. The NAD organized an "Indianapolis Street Dance" march on the streets as the Special School Administrators of Indiana debated mainstreaming all disabled students (the motion did not pass).

At the party that honored Newman's retirement from CSDR in 1988, the emcee asked how many people in the room had learned from Newman. The entire room, filled with three hundred colleagues, friends, and former students, stood up. At the culmination of his two terms as NAD president in 1990, Newman received the Frederick Schreiber Award. Newman also served terms as the chair of the advisory board of the National Center of Deafness at the California State University, Northridge, and as the chair of the advisory board of pre-college programs at Gallaudet University. He wrote a history of NAD presidents, *Sands of Time: NAD Presidents 1880–2002* (NAD Press, 2006).

"I feel my best at conventions and gatherings of deaf people because this is where people, especially my former students, come to me and thank me for the impact I have made in their lives. I get my greatest satisfaction as a role model from former students. One of my former

Brothers Leonard and George, Larry, nephew Arthur. Larry's parents are in front with their great granddaughter.

students told me, 'I got a D from you, but you were my favorite teacher,'" Newman relates.

His greatest legacy may lie, indeed, not in his articles but in his personal relationships with his students and their parents. The best possible rebuttal to "Talk, Talk, Talk, Talk!" was not his response to Dr. Lowell in 1970, but in an article in *The California Palms,* the newsletter at CSDR,[3] that preceded the exchange by four years, in March 1966. He gently advocates parents to develop in their children a love for reading:

> You, the parents, must go all out and give of yourself. First, establish a line of communication. It is the breakdown in communication that contributes to frustration and to retreat. If this is the case, then you must seek out and learn a more flexible means of communication— speech, speechreading, fingerspelling, signs—used in combination or simultaneously for maximum results . . . Please do not let them wait in vain. The best gift you can give your deaf child is the gift of yourself.

3. Eventually reprinted in *The Deaf American* in April 1969.

Part One

ON DEAF EDUCATION

On the Least Restrictive Environment

Larry Newman's legacy is as an outspoken educator for the deaf. His writings and talks engage us directly in a time when "rocking the boat" was seen as the wrong approach towards leadership of the deaf. He argues for best practices in deaf education and offers a unified-field perspective of deaf education by bringing together elements such as communication modes, the need for rehabilitation services, and educational law.

In 1986, the State of California approved a new state policy regarding Least Restrictive Environment (LRE). The newly adopted policy prompted Newman to write a flurry of articles in protest of the guidelines. He knew that administrators would interpret the policy as they saw fit. He would then adopt the issue as his own when he became the president of NAD that summer. Newman's anger at the way this policy was used by state and educational officials nationwide to keep students away from residential school is relevant, especially because many of the issues he brings up, such as the lack of adequate interpreters, still exist today.

During his presidency of NAD, Newman was influential in persuading the Department of Education of the State of California to set forth guidelines on placement. He also advocated for four principles:

- A Free Appropriate Public Education (FAPE), which espoused the slogan "quality education by quality people" as a guiding principle.
- The right of education placement choice for parents and children.
- Support for the role of central school programs.
- Qualified deaf and hard of hearing professionals in education decision and monitoring processes.

In spite of Newman's efforts, the Individuals with Disabilities Education Act (IDEA) and its predecessor, PL 94–142, continue to promote the placement of deaf and hard of hearing students in mainstreamed environments by local education agencies (LEAs). Prior to the passage of the law in 1975, 49 percent of deaf students were enrolled in residential or day schools for deaf students. In the 2006–2007 school year, 71.6 percent of all deaf and hard of hearing students were educated in a regular school setting with hearing students, a self-contained classroom in a regular educational setting, a resource room, or other solutions.[1] More often than not, the LEA has final authority on the placement of the student, not the parent.

Today, the LRE clause lives on as one of the six principles that govern the education of the disabled in IDEA. In the following excerpts of Newman's writings, Newman takes on the special educational establishment by pointing out the irony that deaf schools are considered a least restrictive environment and strives to reframe the definition of LRE.

---

1. Gallaudet Research Institute (December 2006). *Regional and National Summary Report of Data from the 2006–2007 Annual Survey of Deaf and Hard of Hearing Children and Youth.* Washington, DC: GRI, Gallaudet University.

Perspectives — The Most Restrictive Environment

The Least Restrictive Environment (LRE) is often mentioned in relation to PL 94–142 in terms of placement of handicapped students with those who are non-handicapped and in a school near the student's place of residence.[2] This resulted from the reasoning that handicapped children are, first of all, human beings with the same inalienable rights as those who are not segregated or placed in a school far from home. How could anyone dispute this type of logic and the human consideration involved?

I raise my hand.

Surface logic can be highly misleading and what is involved, really, is human inconsideration. What is good for the goose does not necessarily apply to the gander. First of all, those who have different handicaps have different needs. It is inconceivable that blind children can be educated the same way as deaf children or deaf children the same way as severely handicapped children. The educational problems related to sight, sound, or developmental processes are too complex for any one teacher or resource specialist to handle, not to mention the knowledge, the training, the skills that are required.

Secondly, what is really meant by the least restrictive environment? Is it not an environment where an individual can interact with others, can function with a minimum of barriers, can develop not only physically but emotionally and socially?

Let us focus on deaf children. Most of them were born deaf. A large number of 15 to 19 year old deaf students function at the concept level of basic English language of a 6 or 7 year old child. Because of minimum

---

Riverside Palms 27, no. 1 (Winter 1982)

2. The simplest definition of LRE can be found in Statute 20 U. S.C. §1412 (5) (B) of IDEA, which states a strong preference for educating students with disabilities in regular classes with appropriate aids and supports. PL 94–142 is now known as the Individuals with Disabilities Educational Act (IDEA). The term is archaic and is not used anymore.

communication with family members most deaf children have had limited experiences upon which to build their language. Also, visual attentiveness lends itself to fatigue far more than would be the case involving the auditory channel. The implications should be clear in terms of the deaf child's attention span, receptiveness to interpreting services, etc. Because deafness isolates one from the stimulation of people and other elements in the environment, there is to some degree a greater chance of being emotionally and socially maladjusted.

If a continuum were to be drawn up I would place a local public school setting with one or two deaf students in a class as the most restrictive environment. Not far removed from this would be one to three classes for deaf children in a public school. The least restrictive environment would be a state residential school with a comprehensive program followed by a large day school program that has a population large enough to serve students on a K–6 or 7–12 grade level.

Any deaf student who has to learn via an interpreter rather than directly from a teacher is restricted. A deaf student who cannot understand his peers in a classroom is restricted. If a deaf student does not have someone who can communicate with him in order to counsel him and if he has visual and sentence memory problems and there is no one to diagnose them then this student labors under severe constraints. If after school activities such as sports, parties, field trips, scouting are not available to him in a meaningful way then this student is in a most restrictive environment.

It is interesting to note that the term "institutionalized" is often used as the opposite of mainstreaming. It does not take much imagination to realize that the term "institutionalized" carries with it a stigma or sharply negative connotation. It evokes pictures of state hospitals, of people locked away in remote places and removed from society. Unfortunately, students in residential schools are often considered to be "institutionalized" in spite of the fact they are at these schools approximately 180 days or half of a year.

Such sayings as "Beauty is in the eye of the beholder" and "Age is just a state of mind" apply to students in a state school for the deaf. They, in most cases, feel institutionalized when they are *not* in a residential school because with minimal communication outlets and few people who understand them they labor under constraints forced upon them because of their hearing handicap. They are, in effect, institutionalized souls in society's sea of sound.

It is difficult to picture students in state schools being considered institutionalized when there is so much positive human interaction, meaningful learning and extra-curricular activities going on and when, above all, children who formerly were mainstreamed or in small day school programs indicate to us how thankful and happy they are to be in a residential school where it is possible for them to develop a healthy sense of self in an environment which, to them, is the least restrictive.

A point in time comes when the choice by parents must be made on whether their child should be home from school daily or away from home in order to get the best education possible. Parents should be aware that there is a difference between preparing and educating a child to live productively and independently and the pseudo integration that comes from "rubbing elbows" with non-handicapped peers. In this respect I am reminded of Coleridge's line from the *Ancient Mariner*: "Water, water everywhere, not a drop to drink."[3]

The reality of the whole situation was brought home to me when my own deaf daughter asked if she could live in one of the dormitories instead of in our comfortable home with her loving parents. She was having such a good time playing flag football, chatting with her peers, and feeling biological forces stirring within her when her male counterparts asked her to dance or flirted with her.

Is this not the least restrictive environment for my deaf daughter? Is this not what the mainstream of life is all about?

---

3. Samuel Taylor Coleridge, "The Rime of the Ancient Mariner," *Lyrical Ballads, with a Few Other Poems* by William Wordsworth and Samuel Taylor Coleridge (London, 1798).

Considerations to Consider about the Least Restrictive Environment

The Least Restrictive Environment (LRE) is mentioned only once in PL 94–142 yet it is being widely interpreted as the thing to do in terms of school placement, as an end in itself, and as practically a state of the art achievement. The mandates of PL 94–142 were drafted to apply to all handicapped children and not to a specific handicap with unique needs. This generalized approach has resulted in a disruption, if not an upheaval, in the education of the deaf.

What does LRE mean? Exactly what it states or to belabor the point— an environment with the fewest restrictions possible. How do we translate this statement so that it applies to deaf children? The keystone to a deaf child's success in any educational environment is *communication*— first, last and always. A primary requirement then is barrier-free communication which means accessibility to support or related services and after school activities.

What does LRE mean to hearing people who are decision makers or writers of education codes and other rules? It means placement with non-handicapped peers and removal from so-called isolated or segregated facilities. The strong public sentiment—practically an enveloping tide—is for all handicapped children to attend local or neighborhood schools. Non-handicapped children must learn to accept, if not tolerate and get along with handicapped peers. In California, the governor just signed into law a bill that would henceforth prohibit the building of segregated facilities.

Within the vortex of this encroaching tide stand our deaf children. As was mentioned before, there is a blanket approach to their education and, therefore, their school placement. The largely visual processing of deaf children is now being equated with the auditory processing of

NAD Broadcaster 8, no. 10 (November/December 1986)

the blind, the wheelchair bound, the mentally retarded, and those other handicapped children whose hearing is intact.

There is a tremendous difference between visual processing and auditory processing. The offshoot is communication barriers. The deaf child faces such barriers in interactions with teachers in neighborhood schools or mainstream classes, in support or related services such as with the counselor or psychologist, in peer interaction, in after school activities involving sports, student body government, or social affairs.

At this point, it may be interjected that there are interpreters to bridge the gaps. Balderdash! Not only are there not enough qualified interpreters but there is no comparison between direct and indirect communication. What person would want to go to Germany with an interpreter in the classroom practically all his school life? The tone, the emphasis, the eloquence are always lost in translation.

Parents have lost court decisions in what is an appropriate school placement for their children. Even the argument that their children needed a special curriculum, highly trained teachers and different learning materials was curtly dismissed as administrative problems. It is more than an administrative problem. It involves costs, availability of facilities, logistics and a hundred other things.

No wonder we are now seeing classrooms full of deaf children with a wide range in age, from four to twelve years. No wonder we are seeing school programs housing children with different handicaps. Teachers are teaching deaf children in isolated places without supervision, without interaction with colleagues, without the funds to purchase special learning materials.

Frighteningly, the quality of the lives and the destinies of deaf children are determined by the Individual Education Plan (IEP) team which is, more often than not, made up of inexperienced and naïve members. The goals could be set low enough so that parents can be fooled into thinking that they have been met.

If school placement is to be based on the IEP then the approach should be a global one. There should be a variety of equally important school placement options available, not an arbitrary ranking of settings. Every state, city, or county needs a variety of placement options such as residential schools, special classes, hospitals and home teaching, resource rooms, itinerant teachers, integration in public school buildings and mainstreaming in regular grades.

Every state needs quality residential schools for those whose educational, social, and emotional needs cannot be met in other ways. For these children the residential school is and can be the least restrictive environment. This type of placement is singled out here because it is the major one of all the school placement options whose existence is being threatened. When one considers that deafness is a low incidence handicap then residential schools are one of those few types of programs where there is a large enough body of students to offer chronologically age and mentally functioning appropriate grade placement. There is 24-hour communication going on directly from staff instead of indirectly from interpreters. Here there is no need to worry about the shortage of qualified interpreters and the vagaries of their attendance record.

Finally, it cannot be emphasized enough, the key point here is that deaf children should have equal educational opportunities; we must guarantee these children and their parents a full range of educational options specific to their needs. A good education is the birthright of every child and it is not less for a deaf child as he searches for his place in the sun.

Current and Future Trends in the Education of the Hearing Impaired[4]

Newman was a leading force behind a protest outside a national leadership conference where federal education officials addressed the issue of LRE by defending and promoting the concept of placing handicapped children in local public school classrooms. He was giving a speech inside the building while over 150 demonstrators were rallying outside.[5]

It is my understanding that we who are here today represent a wide range of interests and involvement in the well-being of our deaf people: state special education officials, local education agencies, state residential school and day school people, deaf adult consumers, students, parents, and other professionals.

This is marvelous!

Who knows but we can make this day a memorable one. Who knows but we can be the spark that sets in motion forces impacting on the quality of the lives of our deaf people not only in Indiana but perhaps I am starry-eyed—nationwide.

First, I hope to arouse a deeper understanding and sensitivity to what we face as deaf persons. Most of us have learned to adjust to our deafness but there are times when it hangs heavy on us. We need to determine if there are attitudinal and communication barriers before we decide where to work, to live and to retire.

In the area of education we need to look at the big picture. We need to understand why deaf people are concerned about what is happening in the field. We have always had a thirst, a burning desire to learn, and what we are seeking are equal educational opportunities which hearing

---

Talk, National Leadership Conference in Indianapolis, Indiana, May 20, 1987

4. The term *hearing impaired* has fallen out of fashion in describing the deaf community.

5. *NAD Broadcaster* 9, no. 5 (May 1987): 1.

people take for granted. The right to an education did not come easy to us. For example, in the 18th century Jean Massieu from France, the first deaf teacher of deaf students,[6] had this burning desire to learn. He saw neighborhood children going to school and tried to follow them but was forcefully told by his father that he was not educable and his deafness was a punishment from god. He languished until he was 12 years old when, fortunately, he was rescued and tutored by a hearing teacher of deaf students, the Abbe Sicard. In one short year Jean Massieu electrified the academic circles in France by his ability to read and write and by his erudition. He opened the doors for other deaf people to be educated.

Deaf people established 22 schools for deaf students in America and a black man, Andrew Foster,[7] opened several schools for deaf children in many parts of Africa. We fought for the right to use sign language. Many of my friends were hit on the palms of their hands or on their thighs with a ruler or a pointer if they used sign language. If one of my classmates used sign language all of us were made to stand up, raise our arms and close our eyes. For periods of time we were deaf and blind.

Teaching deaf children is a complex undertaking. Not only must one use a different communication mode but one must have insight, special skill and the personality to understand and get along with the deaf child. It is not simply a matter of reading signs or understanding distorted speech— it is the ability to penetrate layer after layer of what appears on the surface. Rejected by neighborhood children at home, living with parents who cannot communicate with them to the same degree and intensity as with hearing siblings, these deaf children come to school lacking a healthy sense of self. They may act out, lash out at you and mutter obscenities. It takes a special person to sidestep all this and give strokes.

Deaf children tell me that their parents are kind enough to take them on outings but they do not explain anything. They do not tell them why

---

6. Newman's references to French educators are probably due to the then-recent publication of *When the Mind Hears* by Harlan Lane (1984), which traced the history of deaf education in America to the education of the deaf in France in the eighteenth century. This book contributed to a resurgence of deaf pride within the community in the 1980s.

7. Andrew Foster (1925–1987) was a deaf African American who established thirty-one schools for the deaf in Africa from 1956 to 1987 before dying in a plane crash. His students continued his work—today there are over 300 schools for the deaf in Africa.

they are getting a divorce. They do not tell them bedtime stories. Siblings become the third parent.

If we can realize that only 10 to 15 percent of learning takes place in the classroom then we can see the wide gaps in a deaf child's total growth. Unless the deaf child is with people who communicate meaningfully with him, practically a whole world of incidental learning bypasses him. The subtleties of language, the shades of meaning are lost. I learned about sex from my peers. I learned about the different cuts of meat from my peers. My parents would do things for me and when it came time to leave the nest, I had a long road to travel in understanding the world around me. I would never have worked for a certain hotel if I knew what the term "restricted clientele" meant. I never would have been embarrassed if I knew that "double breasted" had something to do with a suit and not a woman's bosom.

The basic human needs for social interaction with kindred souls, for psychological security, for understanding and happiness are powerful needs. This is the reason that over 90 percent of us intermarry.[8] This is the reason why we have clubs, churches, state associations, and national organizations for the deaf. This is the reason why we have world games for the deaf and highly attended basketball, softball, bowling tournaments all over America.

A major point I wish to get across to you is that there will be damaging emotional and psychological scars if the social needs of our deaf people are ignored. Forty research studies showed that when the development of social skills are not addressed, handicapped children become poorly accepted, neglected, or socially rejected by their non-handicapped peers as a result of physical placement in regular education classrooms.

The research studies indicated that the majority of handicapped children will always lag behind their non-handicapped peers academically. Repeated failure will result in a poor self image and an exhibition of behaviors to avoid demands placed on them in the regular classroom. Failure avoidance often leads to social withdrawals or acting out.

---

8. Newman probably got this information from Jerome Schein and Marcus Delk's *The Deaf Population of the United States* (Washington DC: National Association of the Deaf, 1974).

Within this background sketch of our humanity, let us take a close and hard look at what is happening in the area of the education of the hearing impaired. Make no mistake about it, it is in a crisis stage. In the past, we dealt alone with the highly specialized field of the education of the deaf. Today there is a generic approach to all handicaps. Lost in this approach is the fact that the deaf and the deaf-blind are the only categories of all handicaps where learning does not take place primarily through hearing. Children with other handicaps may need special help and special approaches but they do not need interpreters and can function within society's world of sound by hearing. Teachers and non-handicapped peers can communicate easily with, for example, the blind and the wheelchair bound. It takes special effort, special training, special understanding of deaf people as a linguistic minority with cultural differences to be able to communicate with the majority of them.

One result of the generic approach to handicaps is the placement of deaf children under the category of the communicatively handicapped. This is a disservice because the learning style and the teaching techniques for the deaf are not the same as they are for the aphasic, the cerebral palsied, the severely language delayed. It is possible for a teacher to earn a certificate in the area of the communicatively handicapped without a course in deaf-related areas and then go on to teach the deaf.

The point here is that we cannot allow the education of the deaf to be lost in a blanket approach to all handicaps. Deafness is a low incidence handicap—a minority within a minority—and it is so easy under block grants or non-categorical funding to allocate crumbs to us or to ignore needed support services.

There is an effort to remove the "special" from special education and to view all special education programs as a bridge to regular school programs. The current public mood is such that isolated and segregated facilities arouse negative feelings. In California a law has been passed that forbids the building of such facilities.

This change in public sentiment—or what has finally come to the surface—is understandable and has some merit. It is an outgrowth of the past evils associated to segregation of blacks and the reluctance of the public to accept in the mainstream children with disabilities or those who are different. Legislators and government people, especially those who themselves have handicapped children,[9] are telling us that it is no longer acceptable to segregate handicapped children. They are telling us that non-handicapped children must learn to get along and interact with those less fortunate than them. Handicapped children must also learn what the real world is like and put up with the slings and arrows.

There is a nationwide effort to put teeth in the mandates of PL 94–142 especially in relation to mainstreaming and the Least Restrictive Environment. PL 94–142, while it has made possible a free and appropriate public education for the benefit of all handicapped children, has really hurt the education of the deaf, primarily because of the way it has been interpreted. The term "Least Restrictive Environment," for example, was mentioned only once, yet look how it has become the thing to do in placement decisions. Ignored is the phrase "commensurate with their needs." Mainstreaming and the Least Restrictive Environment are now on the same pedestal as motherhood and apple pie.

What a Pandora's Box such a term has opened. LRE is interpreted to mean the local or neighborhood school or the mainstream setting. Common sense should tell us that it should be interpreted to mean whatever is least restrictive for a particular handicap—communication accessibility, for example, for deaf children—not distance from home or physical proximity to nonhandicapped peers.

The spirit and intent of the mandates of PL 94–142 have been lost. What has happened to the stipulation that there be a range of school placement options? In the past when parents moved to another state they could enroll their deaf child directly in a school of their choice and they could enroll their child in another district if they did not agree with the philosophical approach in the district of their residence. Today they do not have the school placement options they had before. Sometimes they need to sell their homes in order to be near the school of choice and if they are determined and persistent enough they can seek recourse through costly due process hearings. It is important that parents become sophisticated in the Individual Education Plan (IEP) process. They need

---

9. Newman is referring to Madeleine Will, the Secretary of the Office of Special Education and Rehabilitation Services from 1984–1989, who had a child with Down syndrome. Deaf people felt that her perception of PL 94–142 was skewed because of her stand on issues that would benefit her child over the objections of other disabled groups.

to become aware that a child's goals in the IEP can be set low enough for the child to meet them and thus vindicate a school program's claim that there has been an appropriate placement. Also, the composition of the members of the IEP team should be questioned. With the proliferation of IEP teams, the ranks of knowledgeable and experienced people thin out. The education of the deaf is a highly complex area and it is frightening to contemplate that the quality of the lives and destinies of our deaf children are often in the hands of unsophisticated members of the IEP team.

What we should all push for is the *Most Appropriate Placement* (MAP) for our deaf children. There are some children who can function well in a mainstream setting and there are others who will simply drown. There are some who will need a minimum of support services and others who will need much more. There are those, especially those who are personable or good looking or have well developed communication skills, who can make friends with anyone and thus function well socially. There are hundreds, if not thousands, of others who simply cannot hurdle the communication barriers to attain effective social interaction and satisfaction with hearing peers.

With such a variety of individual needs and skills among our deaf children, it is not my intention to make value judgments. I am saying we should keep a wide range of school placement options open. I am also saying that there should be no arbitrary ranking of school settings. I also feel that we need to define what is appropriate. This term has been misinterpreted and abused because no school will want to lose face and admit they do not have an appropriate program. Thus there have been numerous denials of admittance to other school programs based on an ill-defined meaning of what is appropriate. We need to set up minimum standards that define an appropriate program. Such standards could consist of teacher certification requirements, staff observation and evaluation procedures, class size and age range, number of cases per speech teacher, etc.

In discussing what we should call the most appropriate program we need to study the *standards and guidelines for compliance with federal requirements for the education of the handicapped* which is supposed to be a revision of Manual 10. The following statements are still a sore point:

Each public agency shall insure that handicapped children are educated with children who are not handicapped and that separate schooling or other removal of handicapped children from the regular educational environment occurs only when the nature of severity of the handicap is such that education in regular class with the use of supplementary aids and services cannot be achieved satisfactorily.

In other words there must be a series of failures and a mountain of paperwork before a placement change can be made. The standards and guidelines also state that decisions as to the type of placement that is appropriate must not be based on:

1. Category of handicapping condition
2. Configuration of the service delivery system
3. Availability of educational or related services
4. Availability of space
5. Curriculum content or methods of curriculum delivery

You can see that it does not matter what the handicapping condition is, what the problems are in service delivery, the availability of related services (if no interpreter services are available, then it is too bad), and it does not matter if there is no curriculum for speech and auditory training and for language development. All of this is simply dismissed as administrative problems but we know too well that it is more than that. It is a problem of cost, of logistics, of training and experience. What will happen is that deaf children will be placed in school programs not ready for them. Their educational rights, their needs, even their humanity are put on hold, a case of waiting for Godot.[10] There was flak from all over our field because of such statements yet we were ignored in the pell mell rush to reach the altar of LRE.

The guidelines also mention that each public agency shall insure the participation of each handicapped child in nonacademic and extracurricular services and activities. Will counseling services, athletics, health services, recreational activities, special interest groups or clubs have interpreters? The cost becomes prohibitive and there are by no means enough

---

10. Samuel Beckett, *Waiting for Godot* (New York: Grove Press, 1954), a well-known play in which the two main characters wait for Godot, a character who ultimately never appears.

qualified interpreters. Library services and computer laboratories may be available but can the staff communicate with the deaf child?

Some people think that the presence of interpreters will solve all problems. Who would prefer learning indirectly rather than directly? What hearing child has a third person—an interpreter—in the classroom?

There should be an outcry against the federal guidelines because they are for handicapped children who can hear. A nationwide effort should be made to change some of the wording in PL 94–142.

It is vital that we counteract the guidelines because federal audit teams will visit school programs with one sole purpose in mind—to see if there is compliance with their subjective definition of the mandates, especially in the area of the Least Restrictive Environment. Unfortunately, they are not going to monitor program quality. Our deaf children need better protection and safety valves.

Because of the push to be at a school near one's home there are children placed in a class with an age differential of as much as 4 to 8 years. It is back to the old red schoolhouse. There are classes where deaf children are placed with children who have different disabilities in order for there to be enough warm bodies. There are children vegetating in mainstream settings because of lack of qualified interpreters. There are credentialed teachers who say 10 words and sign only one. There is no supervision or peer sharing of teaching strategies for teachers who have the only class for deaf children in public school settings. Program specialists in the area of deafness in the public school system do not have the power to evaluate teachers or to hire and fire them. They can make recommendations but final decisions are in the hands of the site principal who knows next to nothing about the education of the deaf.

Parents are losing due process hearings because hearing officers have no understanding of the implications or by-product problems of deafness. Are we dealing here with the letter of the law instead of the impact of decisions on the lives of precious human beings? Should not hearing officers have orientation to the nature of deafness?

There are 5 key points I will re-state:

1. The emotional and social needs of our deaf children must be carefully considered;

2. Deaf children should not be swallowed by the generic approach to all handicaps;
3. Attempts to reduce or place roadblocks on alternative school placement options should be opposed;
4. Public school programs should first have the resources, the credentialed staff, guidelines and minimum standards before enrolling deaf children;
5. Most Appropriate Placement should be given primary consideration instead of the Least Restrictive Environment with its unrealistic definitions.

Now, what about the future? What will happen to residential schools? I have with me an article, "The Future Role of Residential Schools for the Visually Impaired Students" by Jonathan C. McIntire.[11] Many of his thoughts apply to us, especially if in the next two or three years there is a continued decline in enrollment. Some of the possibilities are:

- Service to increased numbers of multiply handicapped children, including children who do not have deafness.
- Specialized program offerings.
- A coordinated resource center with the general public education system, for example, residential schools could offer: diagnostic and assessment services, short term intensive instruction in independent living skills, career education, family life, drama, language and reading; vocational training; adult education programs; guidance counseling; transition programs between school and work or school and college.
- Another possibility is the establishment of 5 regionally located residential schools based on the same concept as Kendall Demonstration Elementary School and the Model Secondary School in Washington, DC.

---

11. Jonathan C. McIntire, "The Future Role of Residential Schools for the Visually Impaired Students," *Journal of Visual Impairment and Blindness* 79, no. 4 (April 1985): 161–164.The prospect of educating widespread numbers of blind students in residential facilities still remains elusive. In 2007, 1,160 out of 25,757 visually impaired students were educated in residential facilities nationwide. Source: U.S. Department of Education, Office of Special Education Programs, Data Analysis System (DANS), OMB #1820–0517: "Part B, Individuals with Disabilities Education Act, Implementation of FAPE Requirements," 2007. Data updated as of July 15, 2008.

These are future possibilities, not a wish list of my own. I strongly feel that residential schools should continue to play a vital role in the educational, emotional and social lives of our deaf children.

In your deliberations you may want to consider how the services of public schools and residential schools could be coordinated. Could deaf children from mainstream and integrated settings participate in after school activities at state residential schools? Could there be meaningful reverse mainstreaming where hearing students have orientation to deafness, to the heritage and culture of the deaf and become skilled in manual communication?[12] These hearing students could then be the bridge between the world of sound and the world of silence. They could become advocates for deaf students in mainstream settings.

With the increase of the number of students in public school programs I foresee the need to work closely with community and service agencies for purposes of employment and postsecondary education and delivery of services in a variety of areas such as mental health, guidance counseling, interpreting services, independent living, etc.

What about parents of deaf children? Can parents of deaf children in public school programs get together with parents who have children in state residential schools? This is not only to share thoughts, feelings and experiences but to become involved on a broader scale for the sake of their children who will face an increasingly complex world.

Victor Hugo wrote in 1845: "What matters deafness of the ear, when the mind hears. The one true deafness, the incurable deafness, is that of the mind."[13] The deaf people of America plead with you to open the minds of those who will not hear.

---

12. "The term *manual communication* typically is used in a general sense to refer to all forms of interpersonal communication that depend on visual-spatial use of the body, head, and hands" quote from Marc Marschark, *Psychological Development of Deaf Children*, (Oxford: Oxford University Press, 1993), 24.

13. Hugo, a French novelist, essayist, poet and playwright primarily known as the author of *Les Miserables* and *The Hunchback of Notre Dame*, wrote this in a letter to Ferdinand Berthier, a deaf professor of deaf students, after a judge questioned his ability to teach deaf students, quoted in Harlan Lane, *When the Mind Hears: A History of the Deaf* (New York: Random House, 1984): ix.

Is There a Light at the End of the Tunnel?

Today, in spite of the fact that the education of the deaf has been marred by controversy on methods and techniques of communication, the numbers of deaf people educated, the quality of their education, the diversity of approaches, the sheer weight of research studies are a marvel to behold. Gradually, we have—through CEASD, CED, CAID,[14] and individual independent abilities—established standards for teacher certification, sharing of information of successful projects and programs, meaningful learning materials and devices to the point which have enabled our deaf people to become the best educated, socially sophisticated, and economically advanced of any group of deaf people in the world.

Our historical landscape has been full of potholes, of hills and valleys with struggles to have a flexible means of communication as embodied in the Total Communication philosophy,[15] to have quality education with deaf role models, to start infant preschool programs and parent education. Although there is still a long road to travel, there has been an increase in mental health services, upward mobility in employment, captioned television, telephone accessibility, and so on. The skills and abilities of deaf people have been made visible both on Broadway and Hollywood by the talents of Tony Award winner, Phyllis Frelich and

---

Concluding address, CAID Convention, July 2, 1987, Santa Fe, New Mexico

14. Respectively: the Conference of Educational Administrators of Schools and Programs for the Deaf, the Council on Education of the Deaf, and the Council of American Instructors of the Deaf.

15. Total Communication is an approach to *deaf education* that aims to make use of a number of modes of communication—*signed, oral,* auditory, written and visual aids—depending on the particular needs and abilities of the child. Today, this approach is disdained by advocates of bilingual education. See Ronnie B. Wilbur, "Modality and the Structure of Language: Sign Languages Versus Signed Systems, in *Oxford Handbook of Deaf Studies, Language, and Education (Psychology)*, ed. Mark Marschark and Patricia Elizabeth Spencer (Oxford: Oxford University Press, 2003), 332–346.

Oscar Award winner, Marlee Matlin, one acting in the stage version of *Children of a Lesser God* and the other in the movie version.[16]

Perhaps a lesser god has made us and had not force to shape us as he would, but we have come to a point in time when the light for us glows brightly at the end of the tunnel. We, deaf people, as never before, are living a quality life. Open to us are a broad range of services, taken for granted by those who can hear. But—and this is a strong *but*—we have also come to a point in time when many of our gains are threatened by the interpretation or, rather, the misinterpretation of PL 94–142.

Ironically, PL 94–142 would have been the salvation of our deaf counterparts in Europe way back in the 18th and 19th centuries because of its insistence on a free appropriate public education for all handicapped children. It is still a form of insurance for us deaf people, especially those of us who have additional handicaps, insurance against those who, in ignorance, would deny us an education.

Is there a light at the end of the tunnel? Does it flicker at all or does it glow brightly?

We are in a dark place in the tunnel at this point in time. We have been inundated by an overwhelming tide whose underlying force is its generic approach to all handicaps. The temper of our society is such that educating handicapped children with non-handicapped children is viewed as sacrosanct as motherhood and apple pie.

In spite of it all, I see a flickering light with possibilities to glow brightly. There is a force to be dealt with—the deaf people's historical struggle and need for equal educational opportunities which is denied by the push to phase out Special Education by infusing it into the regular public school. The deaf people's sense of injustice was demonstrated by their march on a national LRE conference funded by the federal government and held in Indianapolis a few weeks ago which attracted media attention to our cause.

---

16. Frelich originated the role of Sarah Norman in the play by Mark Medoff and became the first deaf person to win the Tony Award for Best Actress in 1980. Marlee Matlin played the role in the screen version and became the first deaf person to win the Oscar for Best Actress in 1987.

Now that all is said and done, what then? Are we to become a voice crying in the wilderness?[17] I think there is a chance for our voice to carry reverberations that will hit home.

Other than the awakening of deaf consumers, there are the parents of deaf children. The Law provides for parents to become an integral part of planning for their children's educational future in terms of approving school placements and establishing goals and learning objectives. Parents, as well as deaf consumers, are our key people and the greater the degree of their sophistication the stronger they are as our allies. In California, we saw the depth of their concerns and the extent of their involvement in the formulation of a state-wide parent group with the major goal to develop political sophistication. There are not many legislators that will ignore the cry of parents.

The operative term here is contact with legislators. Congress in its wisdom designed PL 94–142. Is it not time to review, revise or update some parts of this Law? [. . .]

We need to make clear to our legislative people that it is not vested interests that drive us but the strong belief—held by Abbé de L'Epée, Abbé Sicard, Massieu, Clerc[18]—that deaf people are educable and can reach their highest potential in a democratic society under democratic processes.

---

17. From Isaiah 40:2, this reference has unusual poignancy when referring to deaf people.

18. These are the names of noted educators of the deaf at the Institute for the Deaf in Paris. L'Epée founded the Institute, Sicard was his successor, Massieu was a pupil and eventually went on to become the first deaf teacher at the Institute; another student, Clerc, brought the method of sign language instruction to America.

On Teaching Standards and Certification

These columns identify what Newman saw as the most pressing issue at this time in Deaf Education: the use of sign language (referred to here as manual communication). Newman also protested that educators with scant knowledge of deafness ran the majority of training programs. This condition has changed today, for the better.

Teacher Training[19]

Today's teacher preparation programs face a drastically different world: they are more concerned with literacy and have to train teachers how to manage classroom behavior and how to teach in heterogeneous groups, for instance. As Marc Marschark and Patricia Elizabeth Spencer point out in the epilogue of their 2003 Oxford Handbook of Deaf Studies, Language, and Education (Psychology), "Simply put, thus far we have been unable to match the correct teaching methods with students' strengths and weaknesses to raise the literacy bar" (493).

She was an attractive young graduate student of about 23 years of age. Words were forming on her lips but the only one which I could lipread with certainty was the word "problem." After I was introduced to her as a deaf teacher of mathematics it turned out that she was asking if I could help her solve a difficult mathematics problem.

The young lady was a typical member of a teacher training class in the area of the deaf. In two more months she was able to get a degree and to be certified competent to teach in classes for the deaf and hard of hearing. Unable even to communicate with an adult deaf person who has a Master of Arts degree, she illustrates a common but glaring deficiency in current teacher preparation programs: the lack of training in the utilization of different tools of communication to meet the varying receptive and expressive communication skills of deaf students.

[. . .] While the Federal government requires that there be course offerings in audiology, speech, language for the deaf and other auxiliary subjects, no course credit is given and no requirement is made of teacher trainees to acquire skill in manual communication, the basic tool of communication among the deaf. It may not be too far-fetched to parallel this situation with an imaginary circumstance in which American students were given courses in how to teach and then sent to Italy to apply their training minus a knowledge of the Italian language.

The Deaf American (March 1969)

19. *Teacher preparation* is a more commonly used term today.

On many occasions former graduates of training programs have told me that teachers are often given slow students or those with special problems during their first year of employment. Their training has not helped them cope with these types of classes largely because of the communication problem. Frustrated and disgusted many of these teachers have become dropouts from our field of education. The tragedy, one former trainee told me, is that many of them were really fine, talented persons who, if given the proper tools of communication, would have made constructive contributions to the educational progress of deaf students.

The failure of the education of the deaf is causing growing concern. Dr. McCay Vernon, psychologist at the Michael Reese Hospital, in a paper, "Sociological and Psychological Factors Associated with Hearing Loss" (in press), has documented that the educational achievement of the deaf is far behind their level of intelligence.[20] Mentioned were research findings that the educational achievement of 60% of the deaf 16 years or older were at grade level 5.3 or below and that 30% were functionally illiterate.[21]

One condition out of many responsible for this frightening state of affairs is the questionable structure and philosophy of teacher training programs in the area of the deaf. Within a college or university setting there should be a spirit of intellectual curiosity and honesty, of seeking out new ways, new values, new methods. Scholarship of the highest order should be encouraged and pursued. When this has occurred what has emerged are new technologies, new approaches to the solutions of problems that affect the way we live. [. . .]

In contrast, teacher training programs in the area of the deaf are anachronistic. Approaches that might have been suitable 10 or 20 years

---

20. Current studies reinforce the same: "Despite decades of creative efforts, however, deaf children today are still progressing at only a fraction of the rate of hearing peers in learning to read. On average, 18-year-old deaf students leaving high school have reached only a fourth to sixth grade level in reading skills, only about 3% of those 18-year-olds read at a level comparable to 18-year-old hearing readers, and more than 30% of deaf students leave school functionally illiterate," quoted in Michael A. Karchmer and Ross E. Mitchell, "Demographic and Achievement Characteristic of Deaf and Hard of Hearing Students," *Oxford Handbook of Deaf Studies, Language, and Education (Psychology)*, ed. Mark Marschark and Patricia Elizabeth Spencer (Oxford: Oxford University Press, 2003).

21. M. Vernon, "Social and Psychological Factors in Profound Hearing Loss," *Journal of Speech and Hearing* 12 (1969): 541.

ago when a goodly number were adventitiously deaf are still in use now when 95% are prelingually deafened children.[22] What has been done to make allowance for the fact that an increasing number of the deaf are considered to be multiply handicapped? What allowance has been made for the fact that an increasing number of schools are using fingerspelling all the way from the youngest to the oldest students, schools such as the following: California at Riverside, New Mexico, Louisiana, Florida, North Carolina and perhaps a few others? A number of other schools now admit they use fingerspelling in the classroom with all older children, not just slow ones.

One common fallacy of training classes is to mislead students by having them do observation and practice teaching of only the very young deaf children under supervision of those whose experiences have been similarly limited. Primary deaf children are cute and their struggle to speak and lipread is very moving, encouraging and impressive. What a contrast there is when only a few of the older children are shown to be able to write a sentence, read a paragraph, grasp the patterns in a mathematical sequence or speak intelligibly. The fact is that these youth must have more to offer to meet the demands of the workaday world than just the ability to understand such commands as "Show me a ball, Open the door, Jump, jump."

So acute are the learning problems, the language and communication problems, that the enormous complexity of educating deaf children should be recognized and given impetus by having training programs expanded in scope and depth. For example, few, if any, programs have dared experiment with different forms of manual communication, with a way of using it to help develop speech and lipreading skills. No program has attempted to do a follow up on Herbert Kohl's contention that the language of signs should be thought of as a primary language for the deaf with English a second language.[23] No program has been willing to experiment with Boris Morkovin's thesis based on observation in

22. McCay Vernon, "Current Etiological Factors in Deafness," *American Annals of the Deaf* (March 1968).

23. H. R. Kohl, *Language and Education of the Deaf* (New York: Center for Urban Education, 1966).

Russia that a total environment of fingerspelling will mean better ability to think in abstract terms, better skills in speech and language.[24]

What is the primary function of teacher training centers? Simply to turn out speech teachers with a smattering of knowledge about the language problems of the deaf, of the Fitzgerald Key[25] and the Barry Five Slate,[26] or is it to produce teachers who not only can teach but are interested in the deaf, have learned different methods of communication, and thus can communicate with them and understand their problems? Are not the better type of training programs aware of how infinite and varied is the art of teaching, how important the thousand acts of kindness and encouragement, the friendship and support, consideration, inspiration, love bestowed by teachers—the foundation upon which academic success is usually achieved?

In view of the fact that, furtively or not, a large number of deaf children do talk with their hands on and off the grounds of almost all schools for the deaf should it not follow that teachers will be better trained and have a better chance to develop empathy if they knew enough of manual communication to read the thoughts and understand the most elementary needs of growing deaf persons? Teachers who, out of the corners of their eyes, can tell what deaf children are talking about could be in a better position to prevent psychological scars and lessen small hurts that children often unthinkingly inflict on each other. They will be able to direct thoughts in a manner that is both positive and constructive even though the formal use of manual communication is not allowed in the classroom. Since 10% of the parents of deaf children are deaf[27] would it not be helpful

---

24. B. V. Morkovin, "The Role of Language in the Development of the Preschool Deaf Child," *Distinguished Lecture Series in Special Education* (Los Angeles: School of Education, University of Southern California, 1968).

25. A color-coding system of teaching deaf children that is regarded with nostalgia by deaf people.

26. A system that used five large slates to help deaf people learn how to read and write sentences. This method was developed by the Abbé Sicard.

27. This figure is from J. D. Ranier, K. Z. Altshuler, F. J. Kaltman, and W. E. Deming, eds., *Family and Mental Health Problems In a Deaf Population* (New York: New York State Psychiatric Institute, 1963). According to a more recent survey 3.8 percent of all students in primary and secondary schools were reported as having parents who were both deaf or hard of hearing, and 4.4 percent reported having one parent who was deaf or hard of hearing. See Gallaudet Research Institute, *Regional and National Summary Report of Data from the 2006–2007 Annual Survey of Deaf and Hard of Hearing Children and Youth* (Washington, DC: Author, 2006).

to be able to communicate with them in as flexible a manner as possible? What would the reaction of hearing parents be if teachers could not communicate with them? Surely, the teachers' perspective will be broadened if they could communicate with the end results of various educational programs, the deaf adults in the community from whom a great wealth of thought and experience could be drawn.

The point to be made is that the quality of teacher training programs will be improved if manual communication were made an integral part of the course program with full credit given. It will be improved if a required reading list, comprehensive enough to cover different sides of whatever arguments there are and informative on a realistic level, is offered. For example, if there are sample copies of the *Volta Review* so should there be of *The Deaf American*.

It will be improved if the right to dissent becomes an acceptable fact. Trainees should have the freedom to be able to discuss pertinent aspects of a problem freely, to do research work for their theses with less help from the preconceived notions of those who guide them. They should be encouraged to observe and question surface appearances, to think things out for themselves. It would be helpful if they could listen to talks given not only by the members of the Oral Deaf Adults Section of the Alexander Graham Bell Association but also by an overwhelming majority of other members of the deaf community who hold different viewpoints. Deaf teachers, vocational rehabilitation workers, deaf leaders of fraternal, church, club, state and national organizations could be enlisted to give informative talks and acquaint trainees with the thoughts, feelings, problems of the deaf and the services available to them.

While there has been some improvement in now requiring trainees to visit both day and residential schools, much more needs to be done. Visits, lectures, book-learning are not going to give trainees a feel for teaching. They need to serve an internship that encompasses at least a taste of actually teaching not just the youngest but also the oldest students and a trying out of different methods of communication. Trainees could learn from master teachers how to motivate deaf students, how to handle some emotional problems, etc. Role playing with actual problems and situations would be helpful. How would inattention, defeatism, lack of comprehension of words or sentences be handled? Classroom dynamism has long been a neglected art.

Although there are other aspects of teacher training that could stand exploration and evaluation if we are to avoid the continuing meaningless dialogue between deaf student and teacher, enough steps and ideas have been mentioned to do some soul-searching. Deaf students, there should be no argument about this, have a right at least to graduate with an education that is not inferior to that received by their hearing peers.

On Bilingual Education

It seems hard to believe that bilingual education is a popular practice in deaf education today, given the firestorm that surrounded the concept when educators introduced it in the late 1980s and early 1990s. It is even harder to believe that the idea was being floated around as early as 1973, when Newman noted the similarities that deaf students have to Mexican-American students in bilingual programs.

Bilingual Education

The column is relevant because it calls for more research about bilingual education in deaf classrooms during a time when none existed. Later, Newman would come full circle in a column for the NAD Monograph in 1992, in which he elegantly espouses the bilingual method.

One often wonders how to break the cycle of classroom failure in the education of the deaf. Does the answer lie in bilingual teaching? When I read two articles on bilingual education in the Sunday, June 25, 1972, issue of the *Los Angeles Times* I was struck by the similarities in problems faced by those involved in the education of the deaf with that of the Mexican-Americans.

The *Times* article states that Mexican-Americans who have limited or no English-speaking ability have been expected to achieve academically in English. The article further states that the rationale for bilingual teaching is uncomplicated: A child's first schooling should be in his mother tongue and he should be made literate in that language before attempting to learn another.

An administrator of bilingual programs for Los Angeles schools, Mr. Ramiro Garcia, stated that "one of our failures has been taking for granted that a non-English speaking child would be able to learn English and (academic) concepts simultaneously and do it at the same rate and same speed as English speakers."

"What the latter approach in fact has too often produced," adds Garcia, "is a child who falls behind academically as he struggles to learn English—at the same time losing ground in his native language—and who ends up barely functioning in either language."

It was also mentioned in the *Times* article that "Bilingual teaching also sets social and cultural goals for these children ranging from bolstering their self-image to building new appreciation for and pride in their cultural roots."

One who is familiar with the persistent attempts to downgrade manual communication, with the failure to hire deaf teachers for the

---

The Deaf American (May 1973)

early and critical learning period, with the feelings of parents, with the approach taken by teacher training centers, cannot help but be struck by parallel aspects related to Mexican-Americans in the following quotations taken from the same *Times* article:

> The barriers are usually several: finding qualified bilingual teachers, overcoming racial hostility, diverting funds into the purchase of bilingual materials and convincing a school board that teaching in a language other than English is not somehow un-American.

> Sometimes the opposition is from Mexican-American parents themselves, either because of feelings that Spanish is somehow inferior or because of fears that their children will not "make it" in the outside world without learning solely in English.

> Teacher training programs in colleges and universities have been slow to recognize the demand but there are a few now preparing bilingual teachers . . .

> . . . parents whose children are in the programs seemed pleased by their progress, and teachers with experience in bilingualism are usually enthusiastic salesmen for the approach.

The move toward bilingualism in California has not been without its difficult moments, however. Some school systems have compromised on teaching by employing teachers only partially bilingual or not bilingual at all (assuming the presence of a bilingual teacher aide would make up for that shortcoming).

Some systems have not lived up to the spirit of the program, instead rushing their children into nearly total use of English as fast as possible, virtually ignoring the two-language approach.

[. . .] The first alphabet he learns will be in Spanish, he will learn to read and write first in Spanish, and he will listen as his teacher in Spanish introduces a new arithmetic concept for the first time. While this is going on, however, he will also be introduced to English as a second language in carefully paced steps: hearing and speaking it first, then reading and writing . . . much of the teaching is concurrent—the teacher immediately repeating in the second language what he or she has just said in the first language.

"We find," says Ramiro Garcia of Los Angeles city schools, "that children at an early age are very flexible with language learning. They don't recognize the linguistic barriers that we set up as adults."

One Los Angeles principal who has watched the progress of Mexican-American children in her school both before and after the arrival of bilingual instruction thinks the big difference is the pressure that is suddenly removed. She said she watched children grow frustrated and withdrawn under the strain of trying to learn in a language unfamiliar to them, but under bilingualism, "they blossom, they absolutely blossom."

Besides the frustration, bilingual experts argue, Mexican-American children were often made to feel ashamed of their language in school, especially when they were prohibited from using it. That shame, they say, affected the child's whole attitude toward himself and his school, often setting the child on the road to failure.

Thomas Casso, director of Rowland Unified School District's bilingual program, uses the phrase "psychological cripple" to describe the child caught in this dilemma. Bilingual teaching intends to accomplish just the opposite.

Says Mrs. Dolores Allen, a bilingual coordinator at City Terrace School in Los Angeles: "When children feel comfortable about school, they are ready to learn and they take right off."

The *Times* mentioned that bilingual teaching "has quietly been gathering momentum and may be on the verge of major expansion."

Most of us know that manual communication is the native language of the deaf people. It came to be that way because it has more visual surety than any other medium of communication. Many of us deaf people feel that the failure in the education of the deaf can be traced to the failure to accept manual communication as the deaf people's first language and, on this basis, to designate educational programs for them.

Critics of manual methods contend that it is just for a small group of people, that it is not society's language, and that it is too grammatically distorted to be of any value. Such critics miss the many factors involved that give rise to the merits of utilizing manual communication. Of course, the deaf are a small group of people but it is their needs that must be met, not society's. With new signs being created, made possible in today's tolerant atmosphere, and the judicial use of fingerspelling there is much less grammatical distortion. What many critics overlook is the fact that manual communication complements spoken speech. It is able to keep pace with spoken speech which is not grammatically distorted. It reinforces speechreading, enables deaf children to be more aware of spoken language, and gives them a more sure, a more visible input of society's language. More importantly, it is a transference point to society's language in the same way that "Pepin busca la bola" in Spanish becomes "Pepin is looking for the ball" in English.

The sore point is how this transference takes place, its quality and extent. How many times have our answers been ignored when critics say that manual communication has been in existence for generations in many schools with no better results than oral methods? Our answers have always been that manual communication was seldom, if ever, utilized during the critical early learning years. Family involvement was based largely on oral-auditory means. The addition of manual communication during the early learning years both in school and in the home is a phenomenon of the present decade. Such utilization has made possible startling success stories without which there would not have been the great inroads made by total communication throughout our nation.

It would be an uphill battle to implement bilingual teaching in schools and programs for the deaf mainly because too many teachers of young children refuse or feel they are unable to learn manual communication effectively enough. Also, few teacher training programs make mandatory the learning of manual communication skills.

New approaches should be tried in view of the fact that the language, reading and academic achievement levels of deaf school leavers[28] are nothing short of mediocre. There is some doubt as to whether many schools and programs will initiate such a bold move as the full utilization, commitment and support of bilingual teaching.

A course along bilingual lines has been offered and will be offered again by California State University, Northridge this summer. Perhaps other universities will follow suit making it possible for research evidence to become available. Or perhaps the impetus for experimentation along bilingual lines will come from more knowledgeable and informed parent groups aligned with deaf adults who will demand that new ways be tried.

---

28. Graduates

The Bilingual and
Bicultural Approach

In this, the early 90's, we appear to be at a landmark juncture in the history of the education of deaf people. I am not referring to the lingering effects of the attempts at wholesale mainstreaming under the narrow interpretation of LRE which has caused dwindling enrollments at some schools for the deaf but to the fact that we have never had this many—at latest count, 12—deaf people heading schools and programs for deaf children.

In addition, some schools are incorporating a bilingual and bicultural (Bi-Bi) approach in educating deaf children. Essentially the idea is to do what is done in families where there are both deaf children and deaf parents—that is, the intensive and extensive use of American Sign Language (ASL) and the cultural aspects that spring from such a communication mode. This could simply be touching the shoulders to get attention, the use of actions or mannerisms that are a result of being unable to hear or of being visually oriented or making wide use of deaf studies to show the history and accomplishments of deaf people which, in effect, serve as role models.

Empowerment and thus policy decisions have fallen on the shoulders of deaf administrators and deaf program heads. They find themselves, as never before, in the exciting position of shakers and shapers of the minds and overall growth of deaf children.

Not since the 1880 Milan Declaration when it was practically decreed that the full use of the oral approach was the way to go and when deaf teachers were categorically dismissed from schools and programs for the deaf, have deaf people had in their hands a sense of self determination.

Also, rare is the time when deaf teachers were allowed to teach on the pre-school level, let alone the elementary level. Although this unwritten rule is still found to some extent, there are exceptions today on the

---

A Deaf American Monograph 42 (1992)

grounds that to duplicate what happens with deaf children in deaf families, it follows there should be deaf teachers using ASL at the earliest possible time.

The background chorus to the Bi-Bi approach is that with the full use of ASL at the earliest possible time, the minds of deaf children will respond to a facile and guesswork-free mode of communication; that they will be freed from burdens imposed upon them by well meaning hearing educators who feel strongly that hearing aids play a crucial role in the conservation and utilization of residual hearing and in the development of skills in both the expressive and receptive parts of spoken language. The underlying philosophy is that their minds, developed at the earliest possible time, will be so reactive and so alert that they all drink from the springs of knowledge, have a burning desire to learn more and, in time, will transpose their thinking and their knowledge to the English language and, who knows, to the urge and the need to speak.

As a result, the thinking goes, in a meaningful communicating environment, a healthy sense of self, a unique and individual personality will bloom in the same way taken for granted for hearing children who come from stable families and are unburdened by extraneous accoutrements such as speech charts and amplifiers.

No question about it: ASL is considered the native language of deaf people, other than those who have been brought up under aural/oral methods. Although only 10 percent of all deaf children have deaf parents and thus could be considered true native signers, the fact remains that the rest of us pick it up so quickly and with such facility—because it is based on ease of delivery and visual perception—that it immediately becomes an intrinsic part of our lives. Those of us so-called non-natives use ASL so much and so quickly that we become indistinguishable from true native signers.

Make no mistake about it. ASL has no equal as a visual/gestural mode of communication and there are legions of deaf children of deaf parents who are living testimonials to its value as a communication mode per se and as an educational tool.

At this point, am I talking about
some ideal or some Utopia?

Heavy lies the crown on the heads of deaf administrators and advocates of the Bi-Bi approach. For it to be an integral and permanent part of our education landscape, many questions will need to be raised and many issues confronted; otherwise it will as quickly disappear as it came up and will be but a gleam in the dustbin of history.

One paramount question is: Are we moving from one extreme to another, from the aural/oral philosophy to the Bi-Bi approach? Are we saying, as the oralists once did, all must fit into one mold, take it or leave it? Although deaf children are as different as fingerprints and their parents have varying goals, are they to be faced with no other option?

In other words, is deaf John or hard of hearing Jane not to be exposed to speech and speechreading, to the utilization of residual hearing, to fingerspelling? What about modeling or association and transference from one language, ASL, to another, English?

Or will the saving grace be that ASL will be considered a generic term and the teacher will be free to shift from one mode to another within its aegis in accordance to the specific needs of the deaf or hard of hearing child?

What about family members who are non ASL users? Where do they fit in, how will they be sold on ASL and helped to use it?

Surely, from their vantage point as hearing people they have an overriding desire that their children learn to speak. Also, it is an inescapable fact that they wield the greatest influence on the mental, physical, social, and emotional growth of their children.

Then you have hearing teachers who have been in the field for 10, 20, 30 years whose ASL skills range from the fair to the dysfunctional. Of course they will feel threatened and resistant.

A flippant answer: "Remove them" is easier said than done and indicates no experience with union practices or fair labor laws or prior employee evaluation systems.

To where then do the above contrary questions bring us?

It brings us to the fact that we cannot just run helter skelter and hit dead-end streets. It calls for a master plan which includes clearly defined objectives and goals. Such a plan should address the questions raised in this paper. If anything cries out for a government grant, this is it.

It could be argued that others—the aural/oral, the total communication, the cued speech people—just went ahead and did it. Yes, they did and look at the sorry state of education we have today, to quote the primary and inescapable conclusion of the Commission on Education of the Deaf:

> The present status of education for persons who are deaf in the United States is unsatisfactory. Unacceptably so.[29]

The administrator or program head who carefully establishes a pilot Bi-Bi program with a pre and post evaluation system and with enough vision to draw up a master plan that includes short and long range goals will make a great impact on the field of education of deaf children. Of course, some types of progress such as the way the deaf child responds, thinks, shows social maturity, cannot easily be measured. However, one of our technological marvels is the videotape. What more irrefutable proof can there be than living scenes of how our deaf children blossom within a meaningful communicating environment?

ASL might be a given but we must realize that there are other needs. The education of deaf children is far more complex than anyone realizes.

We are on shaky ground when we stipulate that there is one and only one way to go. It is interesting to note that even deaf parents who use ASL sometimes place their deaf children in an oral program. In fact, one deaf family placed one deaf child in an ASL/TC[30] class and another of their deaf children in an oral program.

---

29. The Commission on Education of the Deaf undertook a study in 1988 of the education of deaf individuals. The quote appeared in its report, which suggested 52 actions to be taken that would address the quality of education of deaf people. Commission on Education of the Deaf: Toward Equality; Education of the Deaf. (February 1988).

30. American Sign Language/Total Communication. This was a standard term for a class that used sign language as the primary language of instruction.

Here is an ideal situation where there were options and one deaf family wisely chose that which they felt would meet the individual needs of their children instead of pigeonholing them in one compartment.

Let me make this clear, I am a purveyor of ASL. I have used it with my deaf daughter, in the classroom where I taught for 23 years, in my role as an administrator, in my speaking engagements, in story-telling, in student discipline cases—but never in a rigid sense. And there is no question of ASL's practical value.

The point to be made here—pardon my repetition—is that we do not need to fall back into extremism. Are we not in a more benign and accepting environment? A well-planned professional approach is called for where there is a build-up of data which does not ignore the marvelous variations that are part and parcel of us human beings. Such a build-up of data will, in the long run, be its own best selling point.

On the Residential School

While yet more research is needed fifteen years later, the bilingual approach has become more accepted in the education community today.

The Role of the Residential School in the Educational Well-Being of Deaf Children

This is a bittersweet elegy given at the Wyoming School for the Deaf, especially considering the fact that the school closed in June 2001. Subsequently, in 2003, a study revealed that educational placement settings " . . . account for less than 5% of the difference in achievement, whereas student characteristics account for 25% of the difference, and most of the variance is unaccounted for."[31] So when Newman writes about the primacy of the residential school environment over a mainstreamed setting, we can appreciate his sentiment and nostalgia for a setting that was the source of his greatest learning and the setting where he taught hundreds of students.

I understand there is some controversy going on here related to the possible demise of the Wyoming School for the Deaf. What else is new? Ever since I entered the field of education of the deaf, I have never seen a period when there was no controversy. At first it was a question of which was the better way—the oral method or the total communication procedure. Then there were angry nationwide protest marches by deaf people at various state capitals against what was strongly felt was a misconception and a misinterpretation of the mandates of what was then called PL 94–142, especially in the use of the term "Least Restrictive Environment." Soon afterwards, who can forget the furor caused by the selection of a hearing instead of a deaf president of Gallaudet University. Now we have a split among ourselves related to the use of American Sign Language in infancy and with voice turned off.

Presentation, Casper, Wyoming, November 18, 1992

31. Michael S. Stinson and Thomas N. Kluwin, "Educational Consequences of Alternative School Placements," *Oxford Handbook of Deaf Studies, Language, and Education (Psychology)*, ed. Mark Marschark and Patricia Elizabeth Spencer (Oxford: Oxford University Press, 2003): 52–64.

The California School for the Deaf in Riverside was opened some time in February 1953. What was education of the deaf like in southern California before this school was opened? There were two large day schools and many classes for the deaf—mainly oral—scattered among public schools from the elementary to the high school level.

Mainstreaming deaf students was nothing new. It was in effect before the state residential school opened and still is today. I wish you could have been there with me as I taught Mathematics for 20 years at the residential school. It was a revolutionary change for the students in that for the first time there was a critical mass—over 500 students—and they could participate in a wealth of after school activities from boy and girl scouts through drama presentations to varsity sports. I remember one girl screaming to get my attention when she was told I was deaf. It never occurred to her that there was such a thing as a deaf teacher. This girl later came back to be a teacher at the same school from where she graduated.

The children who came to the Riverside school for the first time were not only starved for an education via teachers they could follow and understand without strain but also for companionship.

I found myself holding an additional period when school was out for there was a bunch of kids so eager to learn and so far back in mathematics. I also remember a group of beautiful and intelligent girls who opted to get married after graduation instead of going on to college. I mention this because it is critical that you understand the repressed normal biological urges these young people had when they were isolated from each other in public schools. It is critical that in the educational well-being of deaf children we take into account their thoughts and feelings and sense of self esteem.

Of course, in Wyoming there is little or no chance for a critical mass. We must, however, keep in perspective by focusing on the educational well-being of deaf children. One way to do this is to ask ourselves what are hearing children getting and why is it that they don't have the same language development problems that deaf children have?

First and foremost, what hearing children have is direct communication with each other and with their teachers they have peer interaction and adult role models. They have communication access in the auditorium, in the library, in all after school activities. Contrast this with what the deaf student goes through. If there is no certified teacher of the

63

deaf, then the interpreter comes into the picture. Indirect communication thus takes place. And this in no way is the same thing as or close to direct communication. In indirect communication there is no eye contact with the teacher, no illustrations on the blackboard with near simultaneous explanations, no time to ask questions in the middle of a sentence. If the site principal knows nothing about sign language, who monitors the skills of the interpreters? If the interpreter is ill and absent or inefficient, will there be other interpreters waiting in the wings? Are there enough interpreters available who are certified or will someone be hired because his or her cousin is deaf?

How is language developed? You can teach the rules of grammar but can you teach language? Language is developed through a form of osmosis, from hearing its flow, from others who model it, from countless opportunities to associate and transfer its meanings, from interaction with peers, from direct communication to what Merv Garretson calls the unwritten curriculum.[32] Through these, hearing students develop language. Indeed, incidental learning plays a large part in the language of hearing students: the chats in the hallways, the voices of adults talking, the dialogue on television and the movies all dovetail to help language grow. In marked contrast, where is the deaf student in this cauldron of bubbling language flow? For all intents and purposes, he or she is likely to be an uncomprehending isolated figure in a sea of hearing people.

Now that all of this is said, where does the state of Wyoming come in where the education of the deaf is concerned? The closest to the ideal of a barrier free environment is the residential school because of long distances from one school district to another, Wyoming has somewhat of a unique problem. But even in California, there is quite a bit of distance in a north-south direction. The California School for the Deaf in Riverside serves students from the border with Mexico to San Luis Obispo. The longest distance from home to the Riverside school is about 250 miles. Students are bused home every weekend and for the students who lived the farthest, we used to fly them home at no cost to the parents.

But in Wyoming the population is much more sparse, therefore the approach must be on a smaller scale. To my way of thinking and

---

32. Merv Garretson, "The Deaf Child and the Unwritten Curriculum," *Directions* 2, no. 4 (1981).

experience, the small Wyoming School for the Deaf seems to be a viable option in view of the options out there. It has valuable support services, certified staff and opportunities for the deaf students to mingle with those who can hear and those who cannot. Although small in number, there are at least other deaf students with whom to develop friendships, share thoughts, hopes and dreams and, of critical importance, a staff they can communicate with directly.

Talking about staff members, if there is only one certified teacher of the deaf in a program, this staff member is sort of isolated because he/ she has no one else with whom to share ideas and help solve problems— no "family support."

The Wyoming School for the Deaf serves as a home base for the deaf children. Although on a smaller scale, the Taft school at Santa Ana, California—when I was principal—had about 100 students from the infant program to the 6th grade. Next door was a public elementary school of about 1,000 hearing students. If our deaf students excelled in math or reading they were mainstreamed with the hearing students for part of the school day. They always had a home school base to come back to for support, for auditory and speech work and for other subjects in which they were not ahead.

Having 5 children of my own, the last one deaf, I can well understand the desire of parents to have their children at home. This is a dilemma that faced many parents at the Riverside school but many of them opted to make a great sacrifice sending their children long distances away for school.

What about cost effectiveness? I find it ironical that we are willing to spend 1.2 billion for a stealth bomber when America's infrastructure and economy are practically in shambles. Ideally, we should not be forced to dwell on which program is more cost effective when future taxpayers and the quality and the well-being of human lives are concerned, whether we like it or not.

No doubt, the larger the number of students in one place the more it is cost effective. However, keep in mind if there were 15 students each on different grade levels and in different programs, the cost becomes exorbitant. It becomes exorbitant if there is to be an appropriate program with the necessary support services as required under the mandates of IDEA. Figure in the cost of the number of interpreters, the teaching aides, the speech therapists, the audiologist, the psychologist who can use sign language. The only way to save costs when students are widely dispersed is to ignore the mandates of the law.

In closing I would like to use a favorite "Dear Abby" anecdote.[33] A wife wrote to Dear Abby stating that she was in a rowboat with her husband and his mother. She decided to ask her husband "Who would you save first—me or your mother—if the rowboat overturned?" Without hesitation, the husband answered, "My mother." The wife wrote to Dear Abby, "What should I do?" Dear Abby answered, "Learn to swim." We deaf people have learned to swim even against overwhelming tides. Dr. Harry Best hit the nail on the head when he wrote in the preface of his book on deafness the following words: "Deaf people are the most misunderstood among men but the gamest of them all."[34]

---

33. A popular newspaper advice columnist.
34. Harry Best, *Deafness and the Deaf in the United States* (New York: Macmillan, 1943).

On the Future of Deaf Education

Newman's optimism for the future of deaf education is apparent throughout his writings and speeches. He imagines the future idyllically and muses on possible strategies.

Throughout Newman's work, a theme remains: his passion for the constant betterment of deaf education. Current research reinforces Newman's assertion that early intervention is necessary: "Evidence suggests that the child's best chances for achieving proficiency in communication, language, and literacy are related to early identification of hearing loss and enrollment in a comprehensive early education program by 6 months of age . . . Family involvement, described, for example, as participation in parent-infant sessions and the effectiveness of parental communication, is essential to the child's early development and is associated with language gains . . ."[35]

---

35. Marilyn Sass-Lehrer and Barbara Bodner-Johnson, "Early Intervention: Current Approaches to Family-Centered Programming," in *Oxford Handbook of Deaf Studies, Language, and Education (Psychology)* ed. Marc Marschark and Patricia Elizabeth Spencer (Oxford: Oxford University Press, 2003).

Deaf Leadership in Education — Past, Present, and Future

Newman made the following presentation at the Leadership Training Program (LTP) at the National Center on Deafness at the California State University, Northridge (CSUN). The LTP proved to be a training ground for countless administrators. Its closure in the early 1980s has led to a change in the landscape of deaf leadership in deaf education.

How It Was

It is a historical fact that deaf leaders were instrumental in establishing schools for the deaf in various parts of our country. Even in Africa the thankless task of paving the way for education of the deaf fell on the shoulders of a black deaf man.[36] We remember the notable deaf teacher Laurent Clerc but at the beginning of the 20th century how many deaf teachers were there? A deaf administrator? The Golden Fleece[37] was easier to find.

In spite of the fact that deaf leaders were involved in and sensitive to the educational needs of their own deaf people, they were pushed aside while others took over what they began. Could the blame be placed on limited opportunities for training in administration? Was the same old rascal, the telephone, used as an excuse? Were interpreters a Rolls Royce luxury? Or was it the Minority Group syndrome—don't bite the hand that feeds you? Most deaf students of this time were the postlingual type. Unheard of were Rubella children and, as for those with additional handicaps, well, God rest their souls.[38]

In plain and simple words, the deaf student already had language, pot was something you put flowers in, Title IX had something to do with

---

Presentation, California State University, Northridge, April 8, 1978

36. A reference to Andrew Foster.

37. An elusive treasure sought out by Jason and the Argonauts in Greek mythology.

38. A possible effect of rubella, commonly known as German measles, is deafness. When an epidemic occurs, deaf schools and programs often see a rise in enrollment.

the descendants of Kings,[39] a glimpse of billowing bloomers were all the chills and thrills for a year. Even under the lousiest conditions and with the lousiest of teachers, the deaf student of that time could still look good. Becoming deaf long after they were born, they still spoke well and learned to write and read by hook or crook. After all, there were blank walls or a picture of grandpa instead of television sets.

Under such circumstances, schools looked good and if a deaf leader emerged and dared raise a finger he would be asked what's your problem, what's eating you, are you a revolutionist?

How It Is

Out of the wasteland, just 3 or 4 deaf teachers rose through the ranks and became an administrator. At social functions he probably had a cocktail in one hand and a cigarette in another in order to blend into the scene. The change cannot be more noticeable than at recent Convention of Executives of American Schools for the Deaf (CEASD) where at least 30 deaf administrators could be counted. Since at least one hand had to be free to communicate it would be interesting to research the utilization rate of a cigarette or a cocktail.

Like Topsy,[40] the National Association of the Deaf, grew and grew. As a representative of deaf people this association was no longer a voice crying in the wilderness. In addition, there was an interplay of forces that helped shape deaf leaders and bring them out of the woods. The hiring policies, the training and outreach programs of such institutions as Gallaudet College,[41] NTID, NYU, and CSUN[42] set an example and had an impact all over the nation. The Center for the Law and the Deaf, the 10 states with commissions on deafness, the American Deafness and Rehabilitation Association, the American Coalition of Citizens with Disabilities, the passage of

---

39. A law that prevents discrimination under any education program or activity on the basis of sex.

40. Topsy is a little girl in the novel *Uncle Tom's Cabin* by Harriet Beecher Stowe (Boston: Jewett and Co., 1852) who grew in height in a short period of time.

41. Now Gallaudet University.

42. National Technical Institute for the Deaf, New York University, and California State University, Northridge.

such legislation such as S504,[43] PL 94–142 all contributed to bring the rights of deaf people into public focus. Deaf people could enter Law or Medical schools. Affirmative action became the battle cry.

One way or another all these forces had an impact on education of the deaf itself. Today can be considered, in terms of deaf leadership, the Golden Age. There are deaf superintendents, assistant superintendents, vice presidents, directors, principals, coordinators, deans of students. There has been a breakthrough in placing deaf teachers on the elementary level and in giving deaf people leadership roles in day school programs. Things are possible now that simply were undreamt of just 10 years ago.

What Will Be

The future is full of imponderables but there is no question that there will be greater demands made on deaf leadership. What, for example, will be the actual impact of PL 94–142? Who is going to see that main-streamed deaf students do not drown? What is going to happen to their social well-being, their healthy sense of self, their ability to find support and reinforcement from their own deaf people? With money flowing to school districts in the years ahead, thanks to PL 94–142, how much of these funds will actually be utilized for the benefit of deaf children? For example, the Taft Hearing Impaired School in Santa Ana serves 13 school districts. As a result, around 100 children from 18-month infants to 12-year old 6th graders are gathered in one place with a large public school of 1000 children next door. This permits partial mainstreaming and reverse mainstreaming but does not take away the role of the school as a home base where speech and language and audiological services are offered. Now, because other districts must serve *all* handicapped children in order to be eligible for PL 94–142 funds, 6 of the 13 districts are planning to form a consortium with the probable result that the Taft H.I. school will shrink and the program become fragmentized.

---

43. Section 504 states, "No otherwise qualified individual with a disability in the United States . . . shall, solely by reason of her or his disability, be excluded from the participation in, be denied the benefits of, or be subjected to discrimination under any program or activity receiving Federal financial assistance or under any program or activity conducted by any Executive agency or by the United States Postal Service." From http://en.wikipedia .org/wiki/Section_504_of_the_Rehabilitation_Act (retrieved March 12, 2009).

In southern California alone there are approximately 145 programs for the deaf and hard of hearing, some as small as 1 class of 2 deaf and 4 hard of hearing students. One cannot help but wonder who effectively monitors these small programs. With the hue and cry that handicapped children should be educated in the least restrictive environment will such programs become more widespread? What will happen to state residential schools for the deaf from where most of us deaf leaders graduated? Will deaf students continue to have a comprehensive high school program?

In the past the needs of deaf leaders in education were: leadership training, willingness on the part of those in positions of power and influence to hire and—confidence enough—to promote deaf educators, affirmative action by deaf people themselves and their advocates, an acceptance of flexible communication methods. Today, to a large extent, all these needs have been met. One heartening example is the action taken by the Santa Ana school district when they hired a deaf principal. Instead of making excuses regarding the telephone and attendance at district meetings, they hired another clerical employee and permitted overtime allowances for an interpreter.

In the future will the needs of deaf leaders be ignored in order to cut costs? Will the struggle to find their place in the sun become more difficult because directors of special education just do not have the time and training to come to grips with the unique and complex problems in our field?

I mentioned earlier that we are in a Golden Age where deaf leadership is concerned. Continued vigilance is the price we must pay to safeguard our gains. Yes, the resources and manpower are here. How we marshal and use them will determine the future well-being of our deaf people.

Inviting Educational Success: A Self-Concept Approach to Teaching and Learning

For far too long education has been considered an *end*. The end is a well-developed human being. Educational institutions are but many means to that end. Educational systems should be designed for students, not administrators, parents, the board, or the faculty.

—Frank Turk, EdD

Ladies and Gentlemen, we have come a long way since the time when we were hidden in shame from the public eye. No less a notable than Aristotle himself made this unbelievably negative statement: "Those who are born deaf all become senseless and incapable of reason."[44]

Would that Aristotle could come back and see what has happened since his time.

Education is to deaf people what the Golden Fleece was to Jason in mythology. He was willing to go through many trials and tribulations because if he could get the Golden Fleece, the throne in the kingdom of Greece would be his. If deaf people could get an education, their minds would be set free and the kingdom of the world would be theirs.

[. . .] Indeed, deaf people have jealously guarded their rights to equal educational opportunities, the same opportunities assumed as their birthright by hearing people.

[. . .] It was a long struggle to communicate the way deaf people wanted, that is, to communicate freely. Now around 80% of the schools in America follow the Total Communication philosophy.[45] Except for a few diehards and sporadic flare-ups, the oral/manual controversy has faded away.

Frank R. Turk, ed., *A Kaleidoscope of Deaf America* (Washington, DC: NAD, 1990)

44. While there are many versions of this statement, the true source of this quote has never been established.

45. I. K. Jordan, G. Gustason, and R. Rosen, "An Update on Communication Trends in Programs for the Deaf," *American Annals of the Deaf* 124 (1979): 350–357.

But other controversies have come into the picture. It makes us wonder if we will ever be free from having to explain, debate, defend, or demonstrate.

Just as we were beginning to enjoy the fruits of our many years of struggle for a good education, just as the quality of our lives improved, there have come dark clouds to bedevil us once again. Segregation has become a dirty word. The blacks have fought against segregation. To people with disabilities—with some exceptions—segregation is like the bubonic plague.

State and other residential schools in various parts of the world are considered segregated institutions, so are large day schools or programs. Governments want to place all handicapped children in the local public schools. It makes sense to them not only because society disapproves of segregation but because it is much cheaper to be "educated" in the local schools. Local public schools are told that they must serve all handicapped children.

There are many things wrong with this movement which is becoming like a tidal wave, sweeping away almost anyone in its path. First, it is not really cheaper. If two or three deaf children in a local school were given a trained teacher, a trained aide, a speech teacher, a psychologist who could sign and other necessary related or support services, it could be very costly.

But more to the point. Why were 24 residential schools established by deaf people? Why is deafness a unique handicap, different from other disabilities? Why did the Conference of Educators and Administrators Serving the Deaf (CEASD) establish teacher and administrator credential standards?

Deafness is a low incidence handicap, less than 2% of all handicaps. Deaf people themselves and their hearing supporters believed in the very beginning that deaf children will need to be gathered in regional programs or center schools in order to have them placed in cognitive and chronological age appropriate classes. Also, in serving a large population, it would be much cheaper to have speech teachers, audiologists, signing psychologists and other support or related services.

Most important of all, deafness is different from many other disabilities because of the communication factor. Like their hearing counterparts, deaf children need peer interaction, role models, after school social, recreational and sports activities. Deaf children would like to be able to talk directly with their teachers, which is taken for granted by hearing children. They would like to go to the librarian or computer specialist and ask questions; they would like to indulge in gossip or small talk with their peers and to have captions on filmstrips, transparencies or film presentations.

Pioneer special educator Dr. Samuel A. Kirk noted that "The important factor to remember in education of deaf children is that their major deficiency is not so much lack of hearing as inability to develop speech and language through the sense of hearing. Their education, therefore, is probably the most technical area in the whole field of special education. It requires more specialized training on the part of the teacher than any other form of education."

And that is why CEASD established teacher credential standards which today are being threatened by the generic approach or by an approach that wants to do away with any kind of special credential because it smacks of separatism.

[. . .] What does the future hold? Because of a blind pursuit to some ideological principle such as the placement of all deaf children with the nonhandicapped—miscalled the least restrictive environment—will there be some lunar wasteland for deaf people? Will there be a multitude of deaf street people and will the words of Aristotle come back to haunt us?

I firmly believe it will not. Such is my faith in the ruggedness and the ability of deaf people to adapt and cope. We will always be in search of some golden fleece.

Who knows but in the future our culture, our way of life, will undergo a drastic upheaval. With advanced technology, more sophisticated cochlear implants or transplants may be commonplace and we finally will become one with the world at large.

In the meantime, in the words of an American patriot, spoken more than 100 years ago still rings true: ". . . eternal vigilance is the price we must pay for our liberty."[46]

AND FOR OUR EDUCATION.

---

46. Wendell Phillips (1811–1884), abolitionist, orator, and columnist for *The Liberator*, in a speech before the Massachusetts Antislavery Society in 1852.

Part Two

ON SHARED
MESSAGES –
COMMUNICATION
AND LANGUAGE

This part offers insights into signed communication and the injustices brought upon the deaf. Newman's work harkens back to the day when trail-blazing educators were also leaders of the deaf community, not only in education but also in varied topics such as sign language and the need for flexibility in communication. In these days, American Sign Language (ASL) was not as predominant as it is today, Oralism was endemic, and Total Communication was a step into extremism. As President of the International Association of Parents of the Deaf (IAPD), he led the organization, composed predominantly of hearing people, to support for the broader cause of sign language.

In 1974, Newman became the principal of the Taft School for the Aurally Handicapped in Santa Ana, California, a position previously occupied by Roy Holcomb, a strong proponent of Total Communication. Because he was an administrator writing about communication modalities in the classroom, Newman struck an unusually deep chord in teachers and administrators of school programs for the deaf. In 1977, Newman took the opportunity to become the Assistant Superintendent at his previous employer, the California School for the Deaf, Riverside.

See! See! See! See!

In 1968, the John Tracy Clinic, a prominent oral education academy in Los Angeles, published a widely disseminated pamphlet that addressed parents of deaf children with the title: "Talk, Talk, Talk, Talk." The materials encouraged parents to continue talking because one day their child would eventually catch on. The following article is Newman's response to that pamphlet, an article that would propel his career as a writer. To this day, it remains Newman's most well-known written work.

In medical terms John had what was called *ophthalmia neonatorum*, an eye infection that left him only 10% vision, mostly in the right eye. The first time John went to school he was amazed to learn that the use of Braille was not only frowned upon but strictly forbidden. "You see," the school people told him, "Braille becomes a crutch and will prevent you from using what residual seeing you have. By leaning on Braille you will be following the line of least resistance."

Words were a blur even when a magazine was held close to his eyes but John did not complain. He had faith in the school officials. Did they not have a lot of experience? And the years they spent in college . . . . What's more their statements sounded so logical such as the following: "This is a seeing world, the kind in which you will have to live. Do seeing people use Braille?" There was even a motto in the principal's office consisting of four words: See! See! See! See!

John's parents were firmly behind the school. Yes, they were 100% behind the school because they wanted John to be as normal as possible. Constant exposure to the world of sight, they learned, was important. They even had special eyeglasses fitted out for their son to help increase the acuity of his remnant sight and to make his drooping eyelids less conspicuous. The school taught him how to lift his drooping eyelids so as to appear as normal as possible.

The Deaf American (October 1968)

No one could say that John did not try. He eventually could make out large letters of the type that are on newspaper headlines. His parents were excited and pleased when John showed them what he could do. The school officials were in a dither at John's achievement. They called in the newspapers and soon his story was carried by the Associated Press throughout the nation. The school took John on many trips to demonstrate his ability especially before the Daughters of——, the Charity——, the Auxiliary Sisters of——. Many were moved to tears and some hugged and kissed John.

Soon something was troubling John. Some of his schoolmates were smuggling in magazines and books in Braille although these were not permitted even outside the classroom. His schoolmates urged John to learn Braille surreptitiously but he refused to be contaminated even though some of the arguments of his classmates carried a more logical ring than that of the school people. One congenitally blind boy told him he had no vision at all so what was he supposed to do? John was flabbergasted because he was told that every blind person has some residual vision that could be utilized no matter how little. The same boy said that if a flashlight was stuck in his eyes he could sense some light but what good would that do. Another girl, an acquired blindness case, said she had some vision left, a small percent, but in 10 years she still could not tell the letters "m" and "n" apart. Sometimes the tail of the "j" appeared faded and it looks like an "I" and the "o" becomes a "p" and vice versa. With a sigh she mentioned that she used to tell a boy and a girl apart but not now anymore.

What shocked John more than anything else was the news John learned via the grapevine that almost all adult blind persons use Braille. He began to waver when he learned that there were some schools where Braille was permitted outside of the classrooms. There were even some schools where it was allowed in the classrooms!

John slowly began to realize how surface appearances could be deceptive. There is a form of eye trouble called conjunctivitis and those who have it are really not blind but part-of-seeing. This type together with those who acquired blindness late in life—and thus could remember many sights and objects, their shape, texture and color—were often used to demonstrate the success of a school's methods. The school's policy and methodology were geared for the benefit of these types. They were often portrayed in the movies and on television and the public was misled. Those who were not in the know or who were fed the pap of exclusively one method looked askance at those who used Braille or could not use their seeing skills. They were considered primitive, backward or just plain dumb.

John began to ask himself what good it would do to read large headlines if he could not read with facility and understanding whole pages which were the heart and soul of what the headlines were screaming about. He began asking himself what does it really take to live in a seeing world—10% sight that stumbles and staggers in trying to visualize things or hands that can make things with consummate skill and a brain so developed that there are reasoning and inventive powers? Which is more important John kept asking himself. Which will better prepare him for a seeing world?

Those school people and his parents, John realized why they have full sight and it is easy for them to tell . . .

"Hey, Bill," John called out to one of his classmates, "take my hand and show me how to distinguish between all these undulating dots." John felt a sense of elation as his fingers moved. "Yes, yes, this is an A—and what?"

"It stands for Alice . . ." [1]

---

1. Alice Cogswell was the first deaf girl taught by Thomas Hopkins Gallaudet.

Reaction to
See! See! See! See! Article

THE CALIFORNIA FORUM
1017 Lido Street
Anaheim, California 92801
13 February 69

My Dear Mr. Newman,

Thanks for your note last week along with a further contribution titled "Teacher Training" for *The California Forum*.

There are two reasons, one minor and one major, why I do not think we shall be able to use your contributions after "See! See! See! See!" This decision has nothing to do with you personally, nor with your English!

The minor reason is the fact that your contributions also appear in *The Deaf American*. Although we did begin the series with "See! x 4," as a bimonthly paper we are easily and progressively overtaken by the monthly *Deaf American*: it is four articles ahead of us now, (we did scoop the monthly with an announcement of your "Teacher of the Year" award) and a reprint in *The California Forum* would be just that—a reprint. Of course, I am assuming all good teachers subscribe to *The Deaf American*, the one and only national publication of its nature.

The major reason, however, is the following from a writer who wishes to remain anonymous at this time. (His letter is hastily written and he wishes to rewrite and polish . . .) I quote:

> . . . What I have to say is slightly critical. I feel guilty about that basically because (of the fact that you seem) willing to give of your own time, talent and energy for no recompense at all to put out The Forum. I also feel that it is a much better Forum than we have ever had before.

The Deaf American (June 1969)

Now for the critical part. It was certainly true, as you admitted in your September–October editorial, that the articles seemed to be heavily weighted in favor of the Anaheim-Riverside School for the Deaf area. Frankly, they also seemed heavily weighted toward a more "manual" point of view. Please understand that I don't object to manual methods (I use fingerspelling as an aid to speech in my own classroom) or to residential schools. I think, however, we ought to make an effort to balance our presentation, more particularly since much more than half of our membership are usually day school (primarily oralist) teachers. Only if we can get them to see one another's views, clearly and dispassionately presented (if that's possible) can teachers on both sides of the ancient controversy begin to learn from one another, respect one another's positions, and maybe even soften up a little on their own views. (That was a heck of a disjointed sentence, but it just came pouring out of my disjointed mind that way.) My main point is that I am afraid that too much of one point of view will only anger a large segment of our teachers. (Solutions!)

I was particularly bothered by the article, "See! See! See! See!" by Lawrence Newman. If you want my honest opinion (which most people don't really want, and few are stupid enough to give, but I'll give it to you anyway and hope that we will still remain friends) I'm afraid that if I am going to be subjected to four more of Mr. Newman's articles, I have grave doubts as to whether I will join C.A.T. next year myself.[2]

It got a very negative reaction from many of my day school friends in this area. When I asked one young new teacher what she thought of it, I remember that she gave me one of those half forced smiles—not wanting to offend—and said, "Well, it was kind of cute." It struck me that perhaps that trite word, "cute" fits pretty well. The article cut in both dictionary senses of the word: 1. clever and 2. *shrewd*. It was cleverly written to be sure, but I carried with it—in the text and between the lines—an insidious message.

The message was very clear. It was that all of you teachers who are trying to get your students to "Talk! Talk! Talk! Talk!" (We all recognized the reference to the old Tracy Clinic maxim) and to Learn! Learn! Learn! Learn! without using any manual assistance are engaged in an

---

2. C.A.T. is shorthand for the California Association of Teachers of the Deaf and Hard of Hearing (C.A.T.D.H.H.).

absurd waste of time akin to trying to teach a blind child to read without the assistance of a tactile aid like Braille.

This allegory could be criticized. No one is asking a deaf child to Hear! Hear! Hear! Hear! and to depend on that method alone for his education. To be a parallel allegory this would have to be the "one-and-only method" akin to asking a blind child to See! See! See! See! and to depend entirely on seeing as the one and only avenue to knowledge.

Well, anyway, the above point is not the important one. Even if the allegory were a good one, I would object to the manner of presentation, (How can I make this clear?)—the **subtle undertone** of both Newman articles (there was another earlier) which said to me, at least, that I should be ashamed of myself for doing what I am doing to deaf children. Of course, this says that I am not a professional; that I just haven't studied the subject, or just don't understand the subject well enough to be doing what I am doing, and that consequently I need someone like Mr. Newman, who is very smart—much smarter than I—and who knows all about teaching the deaf, to come along and bang me over the head with his little teacher education messages from time to time. And if I listen very carefully to the Great One, then I will finally get it through my thick head that the only way to teach deaf kids that makes any sense at all is to use all avenues: speech, fingerspelling, sign language, etc. **This may very well be true!** In fact, I don't even disagree with this conclusion (although many do). It is not that point I object to; it is the manner of presentation. Well, I think I have belabored that point long enough . . . (emphasis in the original)

The above-quoted letter was received after the November–December issue of *The California Forum* was put out, so it had no influence on my decision to leave out your second contribution. In fact, my reasons are stated on page 4 of the issue. The letter, however, had some bearing on the issuance of a smaller and stark January–February newsletter.

I have to agree that *The California Forum* has been slanted, and I think you well agree, too. Here, I must state, for your own information and, since I am printing this letter, for the information of the readers of *The California Forum* that the board members of the C.A.T.D.H.H. have always given me a completely free hand with the editing of the newsletter, so there is no problem of coercion from above. Rather, my problem appears to be lack of commitment from below. As of 25 January '69 we have only 60 members of this Association: that's less than the teaching force in some schools for the deaf!

If I may paraphrase: uneasy shakes the hand that holds the red pencil!

Sincerely,
David A. Anthony
Editor

P.S. If you care to draft a reply to the above, perhaps I'll print it, too.

❀ ❀ ❀

Dear Mr. Anthony,

Your letter filled me with shock and dismay. It was not because of what the day school person had to say but because you allowed your-self to be intimidated by him. You promised to print at least four of my articles and requested that I send in as many more as I could but you announced the change of plans after the third issue came out without giving me a chance to appeal or to discuss the whole matter.

I think you should be filled in on a few facts: You were fully aware that my articles would be printed in *The Deaf American* and although you wanted to print them first this was not of paramount concern at that time. An examination of the first issue will show, anyway, that most of the items were reprints from other sources.

It would be naïve to assume that all good teachers subscribe to *The Deaf American*. Most of us would consider it astounding if at least 1% of the whole teaching force in the area of the deaf in California were subscribers. Which brings me up to a crucial point: Few day school teachers have had the opportunity to read the writings of the adult deaf. Conversely, few of us have the opportunity to express our thoughts in published media that reach day school people. *The Volta Review* is highly biased.[3] My articles may be considered slanted or biased but the *Forum* itself is not. Anyone is free to write a rebuttal. My articles should stand or fall by the analytical writings, rebuttals or evaluations of other profes-sionals. The reader should be given an opportunity to judge, weigh and

---

3. The magazine distributed by the Alexander Graham Bell Association, now called *Volta Voices*.

sift. The deaf student, in the end, will benefit from such airing. After all, what does the word "forum" mean?

You state that the Association now has only 60 members. What is implied is that additional controversial articles would further reduce the number of members. What book or magazine has suffered from controversy? Can it be stated that controversial organizations do not flourish or that only those organizations whose members are in agreement with each other continue to exist? Do you honestly feel that you can hold or increase the ranks of the membership by not printing thought-provoking articles or by not permitting a spokesman to express the sentiments of a segment of the membership?

Have you stopped to study the Convention program to be presented by the Association at San Diego, March 8? I will not go into details but here is a program that is truly slanted. Do you recall the workshop at Santa Barbara? The deaf were lumped together in one or two workshops. There was not one deaf workshop leader. The Alexander Graham Bell Association had their convention in San Francisco. Do you think they would have allowed an interpreter to use the sign language there? In our straitjacket of deafness we have been a patient people. We have not rioted or shouted "Burn, hearie, burn."

Don't you think that a least we are entitled to a page or two to express our thoughts and feelings?

If an association is so weak that it falls apart because of a few articles then let us go out with a bang and not a whimper.

Enclosed you will find my reply to Mr. Anonymous.

Sincerely,
Lawrence Newman

❖ ❖ ❖

Dear Mr. Anonymous,

I wish you would reveal your name so that if we meet I could go over, shake your hands and chat with you. Although I feel you are way off base in your statements about my "See! See! See! See!" article I respect your right to speak up and to differ with me.

First, permit me to refer to your criticism of my approach. I used a satirical approach which, in the annals of literature, has been an effective tool in ameliorating or changing adverse social conditions. There was a famous piece on bad child labor conditions in the early part of this century. If I remember correctly the satire was in verse and there were lines such as "While the child toils and sweats all day, the men on the golf course are at play." Referring to the refusal to serve the Negro people at luncheon counters, satire was used recently by Harry Golden when he said that if we all stood up when being served there would be no problem.

My article was not referring to teachers in particular but to the system as a whole. You realize that today 95% of the deaf school population is prelingually deaf while not too many years ago the postlingually deaf type predominated. A system that permits the same methods to be employed for two diverse deaf population types is absurd. A system that does not make allowance for the increasing number of multiply handicapped deaf children is absurd. A system that is bent on making deaf children pale imitations of hearing children instead of teaching them to accept their deafness and the limitations imposed by it is absurd. A system that represses a deaf child's natural urge to communicate freely, that considers speech and lipreading more important than language and learning is absurd. I was hoping that by satirizing such absurdities we could be provoked, could laugh at ourselves and could try to come down to more sensible and realistic ways of educating the deaf.

I consider the education of the deaf a highly complicated, difficult and trying field. I feel that teachers of the deaf in all types of programs have a frustrating and enormously difficult job and that so many of them are unsung heroes and heroines. It, therefore, was strange to me that you felt I was belittling your type. I consider the teaching of speech and lipreading an indispensable part of a deaf student's total development but I disagree with the extent and the way they are being used. It is ironical the way you feel about my banging you on the head with my "little teacher education messages." No deaf persons run teacher training programs, few are in positions of authority, and yet if an adult deaf person who has experienced a lifetime of deafness dares to put his feelings and thoughts in words you resent it. Your resentment is so great that you threaten to quit our Association. You complain about the "manual slant" while, luckily you do not have to do any lipreading. I choose to call it a slant to reality especially when 73% of the spoken words cannot even be seen on the lips.

You mention the negative reaction to my article you received in your area. At the risk of sounding immodest, I would like to mention some positive reactions I received not only on a local and a state but on a national level. One hearing day school teacher made reprints and mailed them out to parents of deaf children in her area. An administrator of a day school program decided to make it required reading for new teachers in her area. There were requests for reprints from a psychologist in the Midwest and from a school administrator. Another day school teacher liked it enough to ask for three reprints so that she could post it on her bulletin board, pass it around to other teachers and to parents. Most important of all, deaf persons themselves wrote or told me in person how great the article was. The National Association of the Deaf has decided to make the article part of their brochure on lipreading.

My articles should stand or fall by the analytical writings and rebuttals or by the evaluations of my fellow teachers or other professionals. The reader should be given an opportunity to judge, weigh and sift. The deaf student, in the end, stands to benefit.

Sincerely,
Lawrence Newman

P.S. As an after thought and in view of your statement that you could not stand any more of my articles I am taking the liberty of quoting a hearing man from Des Moines, Iowa, a consultant for the deaf and hard of hearing, in regard to one of the articles that was to be printed in the FORUM:

> . . . to comment on your article, "Reality Is Sometimes Funnier than Fiction." It is one of the most humorous and yet touching articles I have ever read on the subject of what it means to be deaf. Although my parents are deaf and I have been around the deaf all my life, I have never before realized the full import of why my mother always has so much loose change in her pocketbook. Because your article provides such excellent insight into deafness, I have taken the liberty of reproducing it and sending it to our counselors in our district offices as an in-service training bulletin . . .

For Thine Is the Power
and the Glory . . .

Communication can take various forms each no less meaningful than the other: a pat on the head that reassures, the signal for okay or the language of the eyes. Need two lovers say more? The hand manipulations of the stock market auctioneer under all the pressure and noise, the attendant on the ground signaling with his hands to the pilot in the cockpit of the airline jet, the hand and body histrionics of the baseball coach giving orders to the batter are each a remarkable testimony to the ingenuity of man. Since the dawn of history whenever there was a need to communicate or to find substitute methods of communication man would find a way.

Any method of hand communication used anywhere, no matter how ingenuous, even those used by Indian tribes, would pale into insignificance when compared to the range, versatility, flexibility and colorfulness of the language of signs used by us deaf people. Who else in this world of ours could use just two hands and make them recite poetry, ring out lines from Shakespeare's plays, make dull prose come alive with rich, descriptive imagery? Who else could from airy nothingness create pictures, spell words, give information, impart knowledge? Who else could make facial expressions—the weavings of the eyebrows, the wrinklings of the nose, the convolutions of the lips—work in synchronization with the hands? This is the miracle that we deaf have wrought, that we have polished and refined (although more could be done) until we can communicate with each other and with an audience instantaneously, clearly and with more than common surety and grace.

Being no exception when it comes to satisfying man's basic need and urge to communicate, to develop himself, to participate in cultural activities, we sought and molded substitute methods of communication for different situations. Because of distance, angular vision, lighting how

The Deaf American (November 1968)

else could we view and follow with understanding dramatic presenta-tions on stage (brought to exquisite perfection and the highest peak of art by the National Theatre of the Deaf)? How else could individual deaf virtuosos infuse rhythm, pitch and tune into poetry and song ren-derings in such a way that an audience of 500 or more could visualize and be stirred as our hearing counterparts are at a songfest? This is the type of signs taken out of common everyday usage and transformed so that it will with a cadence of its own appeal to the eyes of the deaf in the same way that talented voices appeal to the ears.

And there are our own lectures, storytellers, and pantomimes who can hold an audience spellbound with exaggerated body movements, timely pause and emphasis and large movements and convolutions of the arms and hands. On a professional level, born deaf Bernard Bragg using his body, face and hands has been able to communicate to hearing audiences at nightclubs, on television and with one-man stage presentations.

Conferences, workshops, committee, club, state and national associa-tion meetings could never have mushroomed and functioned effectively without the utilization of manual communication. The constitutions of some of these organizations of the deaf must be read to be believed. Their professional style and language, their sheer brilliance could not have been brought to paper without the numerous give and take, made possible by manual communication, of committee and assembly sessions.

Even at the churches the deaf attend the sermons are either delivered or interpreted in the language of signs. Finally, a visit at the home of a typ-ical deaf couple will find them conversing more or less with their hands. Manual communication has been and continues to be used and welcomed at most places where the deaf congregate except where it is needed the most—in many schools, especially the classrooms of the deaf.

At school assembly programs does anyone believe that hearing hand-icapped children of various ages and different levels of maturity can speechread a person or persons speaking or acting on stage? On field trips is the teacher going to bring a blackboard with her? During discus-sions in the classroom will deaf children often be able to follow what is going on with ease and certainty?

We are individuals with varying degrees of hearing loss and speechread-ing skills. If speechreading were truly effective even with the help of a hearing aid, if it came more than halfway close to giving the majority of us deaf persons a tangible means of communication we would not, as we have for a long time, be relying on other avenues of communication. As it is, in using different communication skills we vary them in direct proportion to the success we meet. We are fully aware that the world does not consist of hand-talking people and that it would be to our advantage to use speechreading but we are realistic and are often driven more by necessity than by choice to the use of the language of signs because we are faced daily with the frustrations, difficulties, restrictions and limitations of speechreading. If it were otherwise there would be **no need for captioned films for schools for the deaf, for 95% of us intermarrying**.

This fact should stand out: the deaf want to carry on an effective means of communication no matter how. They have found that the language of signs singly or in combination with any other method makes them feel comfortable and is instantaneously comprehensible in the same way that the spoken word is to those who can hear and Braille to those who cannot see. It has made possible parallel activities enumerated in this paper which hearing persons take for granted.

The language of signs has some faults, for example the same sign is used for different tenses of a verb, but they could easily be corrected if signs were given the study, respect and acceptance they deserve by those who have, more or less, anything to do with the deaf. Most of the controversy, the hostility, the frustrations can be traced to the failure to accept the language of signs as the proud heritage of the deaf and as an indispensable part of total growth for the majority of them.

The language of signs has been left to toss willy-nilly in a sea of ignorance. Seldom has it been appreciated in all its power and glory and seldom has its full potential been explored. It has served the deaf well but what have we done to hold it up in all its splendor to those who do not understand it, do not know how to use it and tend to degenerate it? It seems we take the language of signs for granted as the air we breathe and who would think of defending the air we breathe?

Alas, the air in vast stretches of our cities is fast becoming polluted. Perhaps it is time we took cleansing action, made our presences felt and our "voices" heard throughout the land.

Of Language, Speech,
Speech Reading,
Manual Communication

Manual communication, that is, fingerspelling and signs, has never in educational circles been given the place of respect and importance that it deserves. The stand taken in favor of it has often been apologetic and defensive. The vilification heaped against it, the fact that it has been made a scapegoat for many of our educational ills, have been allowed to continue with little effective opposition.

The rationale for the arguments against manual communication can be narrowed down to two major premises: (1) It will hurt the acquisition of good English and (2) it will hurt the development of speech and lipreading skills.

The first premise, because there is not one iota of proof, is based more on a figment of the imagination than on fact. How can judgment be rendered against something that has never been fully and formally accepted and given a fair trial by authorities in the field of education? Those who fall into the anti-manual communication syndrome can usually be characterized as having little or no understanding of the potential, the flexibility and the versatility of manual communication. It is the unison and totality of methods—speech, fingerspelling, signs—and not their parts that can serve as a powerful tool of communication in the classroom and make possible correct grammatical usage. Deaf students are individuals with different levels of maturity, mental acumen and different stages of readiness. These aspects of human nature should control the interplay of fingerspelling and signs and the degree to which either is used with, of course, the simultaneous utilization of speech.

The potential and flexibility of the language of signs has seldom been more graphically illustrated than by David Anthony and his language

The Deaf American (December 1968)

of signs classes in Anaheim, California. In actual usage were a different sign for such a group of words as: denture, dental, dentist; for past tenses, for "ing" endings, for such verbs as was, is, are. There have been others experimenting with the language of signs so that it will follow the footpaths of proper English usage but the trouble is that the efforts have been isolated rather than concerted and coordinated. Again and again detractors of the language of signs forget that the eyes follow spoken speech with signs coming within the peripheral vision of the deaf. This spoken speech has correct grammatical structure. The combination of manual communication and speech results in less strain for the eyes of the deaf and less emotional tension.

In the development of vocabulary, take the word "crash." How dull it must sound when one hearing person tells another that two automobiles crashed into each other. The language of signs could help show a crunching effect with fenders flying, the shattering and splattering of glass—vroooom! With the hands acting as such a powerful, active, live visual aid the deaf student surely will have a difficult time forgetting the word "crash." Vocabulary leads to sentences and sentences to language flow. When a teacher uses his hands to tell a student we say "How many parts" and not "How much parts" he or she is using the natural language of the deaf, manual communication, to teach English with three dimensional power. When students can express themselves in a medium that is comfortable and adequately meets their needs, an atmosphere is created where it will be possible to stimulate their minds, and other aspects of their development as human beings.

Like their hearing counterparts, deaf children are enraptured by storytelling but how many of them have really had the chance to "listen" to one? Manual communication can help dramatize stories as no other medium can and this in turn could whet the appetites of deaf children and lead them on to reading where lies the greatest single factor in their potential mental development and language flow. The need for reading is far more acute with the deaf than with any other group of people with the exception of the deaf-blind but, unfortunately, so few of the deaf can be considered readers.

It is understandable the way those involved in the education of the deaf become overly concerned in regard to the second promise, in regard to having the deaf talk and lipread. The feeling is strong that the deaf would not be far removed from the mainstream of society if they could approximate the communication media employed by those who can hear. To bring this about the environment must be strictly oral, they reason, otherwise success cannot be achieved. Under observation and research this line of reasoning will not hold water. First, in a strictly oral environment the individuality of the deaf in a democratic society is not acknowledged. There is a presupposition that all—the slow-learners, the multiply handicapped, those with defective vision—have equal skill and an aptitude for one method of communication. The deaf are made to toe the line under the strictures of one method, otherwise things are made unpleasant for them. Any business enterprise would fail if there were not cost analysis to determine the success of the endeavor. At schools where a strict oral policy is followed can it honestly be said or proved that their graduates have functional speech and lipreading abilities? Can it truly be said and proved that their skills are superior to those graduates of schools where such strictness is not observed? Before any claims are made, have students been screened for age of onset of deafness, residual hearing, post or prelingual deafness and so on? Is it realized that the speech the teachers and parents understand is seldom understood by the public. In other words, when it is said that he or she has good speech the meaning is good speech for a deaf person. Is it not significant that with what little research already undertaken it has been shown that deaf children of deaf parents (where the language of signs is a natural part of communication) have as good speech and lipreading abilities as deaf children of hearing parents?

Then there is the question of priorities. Surely, our primary concern should be with what a person has to say rather than with how he says it. To develop speech and lipreading abilities there must be sessions of imitation and repetition which are more conducive to mental stagnation than to mental development. Has not the cart been put before the horse by the insistence on speech first instead of language? Given a feel for language would not a deaf person eventually want to find different out-lets for thoughts and feelings welling up inside? In fact, would there not be a readiness for speech and lipreading after language has been given a chance to sprout some roots?

Does this imply that since teaching speech and lipreading usurps too much time we should do away with them? Not at all. What is needed is a new approach. We must stop thinking in terms of a dichotomy between the oral and the manual methods because they can be made to work together for the benefit of the deaf. Have we not overlooked the fact that manual communication, if accepted and utilized early enough, could serve as a powerful tool to foster speech and lipreading skills? It could be instrumental in giving a deaf child a larger vocabulary and the larger the vocabulary the greater the chance to recognize words on the lips. Would not a teacher who forms with his fingers the letter "k" and tells a child this is how you begin to say the word "cow" be a more effective speech teacher? Would not a teacher who uses his hands to say "O Little Town of Bethlehem" motivate children who now know exactly what is wanted to follow her and use their voices in singing? Not only is there an aura of relaxation when a flexible method of communication is allowed but such topics as the importance of speech, inflection, breath control could be freely discussed with less vagueness or ambiguity.

A glance at a list of research papers on the deaf will show topics predominately concerned with speech and auditory aspects of deafness. What is needed are experiments and research to show the potential far-reaching role manual communication, when utilized properly, can play in the development of language, speech and lipreading skills for the majority of the deaf.

On the John Tracy Clinic

There is no preschool program in this country that is as world famous as the John Tracy Clinic. The correspondence of this clinic sometimes reaches a staggering 1,700 letters per month and there is no question but that some service has been contributed to parents of deaf children. Because of the clinic some of the parents have come to know each other, which is helpful. There is less of the sense of aloneness and helplessness and parents are given something to hang on to between the time they find out the child is deaf and the time they can get him into a school. Sometimes it is more difficult to be a hearing parent of a deaf child than it is to be the deaf child.

The John Tracy Clinic, named after her deaf son, was an outgrowth of Mrs. Spencer Tracy's feelings about her own child. Dr. Edgar Lowell, its administrator, is a scholarly, erudite, affable person highly spoken of by deaf adults who have come to know him. Both Mrs. Tracy and Dr. Lowell were instrumental in the establishment of the invaluable Leadership Training Program in the Area of the Deaf at San Fernando Valley State College.

While the John Tracy Clinic has made life easier for some parents and their deaf children, this has not been the case for others. Because deaf children are individuals with varying needs and varying stages of readiness, because communication itself is a complicated process, because the children are placed in a situation that lacks flexibility of approach, the needs of many of them have remained unmet. In fact, the high hopes and expectations of some parents have given way to frustration and a sense of failure when they found they were unable to communicate effectively with their children using the Tracy approach.

In terms of the larger picture, where fuller educational, psychological and social developments are concerned, there is nagging evidence that only minimal needs have been met. Keeping in mind that the preschool years are critical in child development, one needs only to evaluate the

The Deaf American (April 1970)

language and reading abilities of the older deaf. Also, an examination of the type, degree and quality of communication taking place between parent and deaf child will reveal one of the many reasons for the mediocre educational status of the deaf.

Needless to say, the minds of all civilized people are reached by communication in one form or another. When one of the five senses is no longer functioning substitutes are sought to fill the void. The deaf themselves have found that manual communication is the greatest substitute available. Unfortunately, manual communication has come to be, in the minds of many hearing people, a threat to the development of speech and speechreading skills. In the absence of one iota of proof, such a fear remains but a theoretical assumption.

It is critical that we differentiate between the communication itself and one aspect of it—speech and speechreading. Deaf children should have to the extent possible the same easy and spontaneous flow of communication that hearing children have. They should be reassured at bedtime without always having to struggle to identify and then to comprehend what is said. They should be able to recognize incidental communication going on at varying distances, at different angles and under changing conditions of light and shadow. To be deaf is frustrating enough without having to add artificial restraints on communication. Without such restraints communication becomes vibrant and meaningful.

In view of the fact that the influential Tracy Clinic's methods are emulated in other preschool clinics throughout the country, one can imagine the positive, far-reaching consequences that will result if the John Tracy Clinic would attempt to utilize a more flexible approach and become innovative and experimental in order to reach the minds of deaf children.

To take such a step would call for action that in some circles might be termed heresy. First of all, an effort should be made to move away from any attempt to make a hearing child out of a deaf child for that is what an overemphasis on speech and speechreading does. The earlier the child learns to accept his deafness and the limitations imposed by it the better it will be for his mental health and emotional well being. Acceptance of their child's deafness should also be part of parent education and they should learn to accept and use manual methods of communication as one of the tools of communication. Parents should be introduced to speaking deaf adults who have used manual communication all their lives as well as to those who have not. They should be made aware that while speech and speechreading and the utilization of residual hearing are important components of a deaf child's total development, they are not the most important. Since deafness is more of an educational than a physical handicap, it is of more consequence that every attempt be made to see that the deaf child develops into an educated human being.

Working from the fact that the child is deaf and therefore must use his eyes more, perhaps, than any other human being on earth, another element of communication with preschoolers should be introduced—manual communication. What is not realized is that manual communication opens a wider door of the deaf child's mind. Moving hands take up a larger spatial region than lips and this is easy on a small child's eyes. When one is deaf, one's eyes search for symbols of meaning. The more interesting and attractive the symbols the greater the chance that one will try to identify and associate such symbols with the world around him. Manual communication, because of its flexibility, colorfulness and three-dimensional appearance, can act as a lever to turn the wheels in a deaf child's mind. It can act as a vehicle to arouse a deaf child's curiosity and lead him to the printed words (hands that portray a tiger is but one step removed from a picture of it and the word), thus giving him the vocabulary with which to speechread and to speak. This is a far cry from being told what to say and do and to imitate, parrotlike, what is said.

A poet once wrote, "The child is father of the man . . ." Too many in our field concentrate on the child without bothering to find out how the man—the overwhelming majority, that is—turns out. The parents and the staff of the Tracy Clinic would gain greater perspective and a greater sense of reality if deaf adults who graduated from different school programs were invited to associate with and address them, if pains were taken to see that deaf parents of deaf children were supplied with interpreters and invited to attend the clinic with their preschool children.

Is it not now time for the John Tracy Clinic to develop a more flexible approach? Unlike the recent past there are more multiply handicapped, and the great majority of the deaf are prelingually deaf. Most of them will always have "deaf speech" and they will always be limited in what they can speechread. If it is possible for a segment of deaf children of deaf parents to have as good speech as deaf children of hearing parents and to be superior in academic achievement, what would happen if all the resources of the clinic were harnessed so that manual communication formally becomes a vehicle not only to transmit knowledge and to overcome the tendency of many parents to oversimplify and communicate only what is superficial or absolutely necessary but to foster speech and speechreading skills!

The John Tracy Clinic, because of its wide influence and because it deals with the critical, preschool years of the deaf, will by introducing a flexible method of communication in addition to its incomparable speech, speechreading, and auditory training be taking one small step themselves, a giant leap for the deaf child and for all of us.

❅ ❅ ❅

February 9, 1970

Larry Newman has invited me to reply to his article about the John Tracy Clinic. Ordinarily I would decline, because I resolved a number of years ago to stop wasting my energy on the old oral-manual controversy. It is not that I dislike controversy, it's just that the arguments of today seem so inept when contrasted with the really grand exchanges between Heinicke and de l'Epee or between Bell and Gallaudet. If the eloquent arguments of those earlier days failed to change people's minds about the relative merits of the two systems, I sincerely doubt that our present day efforts will succeed. I resolved to spend my energies in doing a better job with our chosen method.

In this case, Larry has forced me to reply because he has said so many nice things about the Clinic that I have to agree with him. In essence, Larry is suggesting that Clinic become more flexible, which for him means teaching manual communication. This might not be such a bad idea, but not necessarily for the reasons Larry seems to be implying in his article. Communication should be our major goal. The method we use to achieve communication is a matter of individual preference, and I would defend anyone's right to choose either method. Instead we frequently fall into the trap over generalizing as though things could not be black or white.

For example, I am an oralist but that does not mean that I think all oral education is good and all manual education is bad. I would much prefer to have my child taught by a good manual teacher like Larry Newman, "California's Teacher of the Year," than I would by some of the poor oral teachers that I have observed. I am an oralist, but this does not mean that I am opposed to manualism. Some of you know that Ralph Hoag and I were responsible for the founding of the Registry of Interpreters. I don't know what better evidence I could offer of how important I think manual communication can be. I am an oralist, but I do not think that all deaf children will succeed with an oral education, just as I do not think that all will succeed with a manual education either. In fact, a great many hearing children do not succeed in hearing schools, if we can believe the dropout figures. I quite agree with Larry that most of our oral graduates will have "deaf speech" and there will be a limitation on what they can speech read. They will, however, be able to communicate quite well with their family, close friends and business acquaintances. They will also be able to communicate, even though imperfectly, with those hearing people who are not fortunate enough to understand manual communication.

I do not think that oralism should be blamed for the generally unsatisfactory educational performance of our young deaf students. None of us can be proud of all our results, but to assume that all of the educational problems of the deaf can be laid to oralism is patently ridiculous.

Arguments concerning the superior academic performance of deaf children trained on manual communication from birth does not surprise me at all. Most of them had deaf parents. Who could better appreciate the importance of early language development than a deaf parent? I would bet on them every time, regardless of the method of communication used.

I am not impressed with arguments that parents are frustrated and feel a sense of failure when their child fails in the oral method. All parents, whether their children are hearing or deaf, are in for a good deal of frustration and disappointment. Perhaps they always have been; as I recall, Adam was terribly disappointed with the way Cain was treating Abel. It is not that I am insensitive to parental disappointment, I just want to put down the notion that the oral method is to blame for all the disappointments and frustrations of the parents of deaf children.

Larry is suggesting that we take a "giant leap forward" with manual communication. Others say it can be done with a hearing aid, and still others say, "cued speech." If you didn't watch carefully, you could spend all of your time doing what others wanted you to. We instead have chosen to concentrate on trying to improve our work with young deaf children and their parents. We know that it works with some. If we can improve our techniques, perhaps it will work for others.

I don't think for a moment that what I have said has made the slightest impression on anyone who has already developed his own conviction about deaf communication. I don't think it should, but perhaps it has suggested that the issues may not all be black and white, and that each of us ought to be allowed to continue doing our very best at the work we believe in, rather than trying to convince the rest of the world we are right.

Dr. Edgar L. Lowell

❊ ❊ ❊

5445 Via San Jacinto
Riverside, California

March 26, 1970

Dr. Edgar L. Lowell, Administrator
John Tracy Clinic

Dear Dr. Lowell:

Thank you for the nice letter. I appreciate the time you took to discuss my article. There are several statements you made that need to be discussed further. I hope you will forgive me if I appear to be emotional which in professional circles is considered sinful. It is far easier, in a parallel sense, for a white man to be less emotional than a black person who has gone without a decent meal for several days.

The basic issue in the field of deafness is communication. To pass it off as "an old controversy" or as a "matter of philosophy" is to avoid coming to grips with this basic issue. The grand exchanges between Heinicke and de l'Epée or between Bell and Gallaudet were based on rhetoric. I have tried to make statements based on documented data such as the research of Stuckless, Birch, Meadow, Denton, Hester, Montgomery, Morokovin, Vernon, Quigley, Frisina and Stevenson and on the psychiatric opinions of Mindel Schlesinger, the reporting of Ridgeway, Kenny, Kohl.[4]

It should be realized that choosing the "oral" method for the deaf is like choosing the "sighted" method for the blind. In actuality, there is no "choice." Moreover, what choice do the parents at your clinic and the 1,700 parents in the correspondence course have? Freshly stunned by their child's handicap, a handicap that is incomprehensible to them, they are at the mercy of the "Tracy" name. To them, things are black and white, not the graduations of gray we who are couched in deafness 24 hours a day have come to know. What options or alternatives do the little deaf children have? They have to wait until they are grown before their cry is heard. The choice, really, is not between oralism and manualism because there is no such thing as manualism in educational circles. The choice is between one method alone where things are black and white and the use of all methods which take into account the various hues of one's individuality. There is not one iota of proof that rigid adherence to the "oral" method will enable one to communicate with family, close friends and business acquaintances any better than can be done under the method of total communication. The latter lends itself to an atmosphere of relaxation and comfort for the deaf child himself. In addition, the overriding consideration should be the development of minds so that there will be something to communicate.

The ability to communicate is what separates us from the beasts. There is an illusion of communication when a deaf child imitates the word "ball" or follows the command "to jump." Since the oral method is in almost total use during the critical preschool years this means there is in actuality little or no effective communication going on. Under such circumstances any human being would wither on the vine. Therefore most of our educational problems must be laid on the doorstep of trying to use the "sighted method for the blind." Every time other methods are employed academic achievement shows dramatic gains.

---

4. Newman is referring to previous columns where he has referred to the research of the names here.

The fact that deaf children of deaf parents show superior academic achievement is not simply because deaf parents appreciate the importance of early language development. Few deaf parents can write a grammatically correct sentence, 30% of them are functionally illiterate, 60% of them have an educational achievement of fifth grade or below. It is all the more remarkable that deaf children of deaf parents are superior academically. It is all the more remarkable for a simple reason: they are in an environment where communication is definite, specific and visible. The point to be brought up is that if educators accepted this fact, if the Tracy Clinic would make use of this fact then deaf children will finally be educated early enough by people who do not have language and reading problems.

The fact that all parents experience frustration is no defense for adding to the frustration one hundredfold. . . .

Finally, "the leap forward" resulting from the use of total communication is documented. It is not a matter of "what others want" but what facts dictate. Contextual clues, picture clues, configuration, phonics, phonetics are all used to teach reading. The least that can be done is to try total communication out at the Tracy Clinic thus making available additional evidence for reinforcement or rebuttal of prior research findings.

Sincerely,
Lawrence Newman

Total Communication

Many persons have credited Roy K. Holcomb with being the father of total communication. Mr. Holcomb, who is coordinator of the Madison Day School for the Deaf located in Santa Ana, California,[5] once mentioned that the idea for the term "total communication" came to him when he noticed the term "total discounts" being used in advertisements by supermarket chains. After he helped to start, use, and popularize total communication, various attempts were made to define the term and there have been reactions that bordered on outright rejection to outright acceptance.

Total communication was considered to be old clothes under a new disguise, a placebo, an updated version of the simultaneous method, a right, a philosophy or something that existed for many years but now is being given formal recognition.

Questions were raised on the feasibility of hiring deaf teachers since total communication included speech and auditory training without, ironically, taking into account the fact that it also included manual communication, a skill in which many hearing educators are not proficient.

All this serves to point out the danger of allowing oneself to fall into semantic booby traps. Too easily lost can be the spirit and the philosophy behind the concept of total communication. It has long been recognized that hearing children are not all alike and that methods or systems that are tailored to their needs work best. It has been known that when hearing children such as the blacks and the Chicanos are forced to fit into a school's system of educating whites a lot of time and effort go to waste.

Total communication then should be looked upon as a right or a philosophy whose basic premise is the belief that each deaf child is as much an individual as any hearing child. Its major thrust depends on a multi-approach concept to meet the individual needs of the deaf child. The

The Deaf American (December 1971)

5. Later the Taft School for the Aurally Handicapped, where Newman would come to serve as a principal.

concept of total communication moves in concert to the dynamics of normal human development and to basic principles of learning.

As a subset of the philosophy of total communication we have various modes of communication and combination of modes. In single fashion they could be listed as follows:

a. Reading
b. Writing
c. Speech
d. Speechreading
e. Auditory understanding
f. Fingerspelling
g. The language of signs
h. Others

By including the above I have left an out for those who may want to have visual aids listed or who may feel the list is not comprehensive enough. The point to be made here is: let us not get bogged down in trees of definitions that we lose sight of the forest.

To what degree the above modes are to be used, singly or in combination, is open to argument and to research undertakings. Suppose that some time in the future a research project indicates that total communication is a failure in the sense that deaf children still do not have language and speech skills, what then? Will it be the fault of the type of communication modes and the degree to which they were utilized or to the philosophy of total communication itself? The difference is crucial and should be clearly distinguished. There may be nothing wrong with the philosophy itself but a lot of things wrong with the mechanics of carrying it out. To give one example, a teacher might use only one sign while speaking ten words orally.

Now, let us examine and discuss some of the arguments presented by those who completely reject the philosophy of total communication. "Incompatibility" is the word they use. What is meant is that speech, speechreading and auditory skills cannot develop and flourish whenever talking with the hands is permitted. Research findings which showed that the use of manual communication does not have a negative effect on the development of speech and speechreading skills were either rejected or considered not valid. Lately, there have been more research studies that further strengthens the contention that sign language has its place in the educational setup, i.e., "Sign Language Acquisition and the Teaching of Deaf Children,"[6] "Language Acquisition of Young Deaf Children, A Pilot Study,"[7] "Deafness and Mental Health: A Development Approach,"[8] and "A Program for Preschool Deaf Children Utilizing Signs and Oral Methods Combined."[9] Undoubtedly, these studies will also be considered to have no validity.

Instead of indulging in drawn-out arguments, this question should be posed: What research findings are there which support the argument that the permissive utilization of manual communication is incompatible with the development of speech and speechreading skills? For generations the oral method has been allowed to flourish, as if it were something sacrosanct, without any research undertakings to verify its effectiveness or whether it was producing the results claimed by its proponents. No one has bothered to investigate whether the oral method is compatible with social, psychological or emotional growth.

If things did not work out, that is, if the end product—the deaf adult—showed poor language and speech skills then it was rationalized that the problem was caused by some inherent factor of deafness itself—the price that must be paid for being deaf. On the other hand, if manual communication was used, this highly visible method was easily made the scapegoat.

The statement is often made that total communication is nothing but the old simultaneous method. This can turn out to be a misleading verbal smokescreen for those who do not look beyond surface appearances.

For example, it is often stated that the oral method should be tried first and if there is failure then other methods should be tried but only as a last resort. Thus a history of failure was ensured for those taking up

6. A. Circourel, J. and Boese, "Sign Language Acquisition and the Teaching of Deaf Children," in *The Functions of Language: An Anthropological and Psychological Approach*, ed. Dell Humes, Courtney Cazden, and Vera John (New York: Teachers College Press, 1972).

7. Ann Pitzer, "Language Acquisition of Young Deaf Children, A Pilot Study," master's thesis, Spring 1969, University of Minnesota.

8. H. Schlesinger and K. Meadow, "Deafness and Mental Health: A Developmental Approach," in *Deafness and Mental Health: The Developmental Years* (San Francisco: Langley Porter Neuropsychiatric Institute): 163–164.

9. R. Brill and J. Fahey, "A Program for Preschool Deaf Children Utilizing Signs and Oral Methods Combined," *Exceptional Children*.

the simultaneous method. When a person has continually faced failure it becomes difficult to overcome the negative psychological and emotional factors involved. What is different now—and this is the crux of the matter—total communication is being used at once during the preschool years and in the home as well as in the school.

Under the philosophy of total communication the major communication mode will and should be the simultaneous method because it comes closer to satisfying the needs of the greatest number than any other method. But it is, it must be emphasized, not restricted to this method alone. At certain periods of auditory training it is sometimes best that no manual communication be utilized. In speech and speechreading practice sessions one can alternate from signs alone to explain what is wanted and what is meant to speech and speechreading alone for the sake of practice. During story hour the utilization of the language of signs alone is often highly effective.

It is the total school program, the type of deaf person and his total environment that must be taken into consideration. For example, what method of communication is best for the multiply handicapped or the hard of hearing? What method is best during guidance counseling, at athletic activities or for social hall programs?

The concept of flexibility is inherent in the philosophy of total communication and this is its greatest appeal. That is why it is making inroads in schools and programs for the deaf. Never before have we had a chance to study at different places the results of the utilization of total communication during the preschool years. Never before has manual communication been accepted and allowed to bask in a non-threatening environment thus making it possible to break away from its shackles and to develop and expand in many directions.

Total communication could not have lasted and gathered momentum and strength if positive results were not immediately forthcoming. Parents are the ones who can see and have seen personality, emotional and intellectual changes for the better developing in their children. Never before have so many gone all out to learn manual communication and to use it with their preschool children with startling results. They have gone all out because they tried the oral method alone and met failure and frustration. Their children were becoming strangers in their own house. These parents have discovered for themselves that it has not been incompatible for different modes of communication to co-exist.

Parents and educators who see that total communication is used early enough and in the home as well as in school will be its greatest source of strength. If pains are taken to see that oral-auditory methods are not neglected and that such skills can be acquired while co-existing with manual communication, the trend of total communication will be unmistakable—what is now a ripple will eventually become an unstoppable tide.

Talk at Registry of Interpreters Workshop

In 1972, sign language interpreting was a nascent field. The Registry of Inter-
preters of the Deaf had just incorporated. Newman's prescient talk here shows
the gratitude that the deaf person has for the interpreters, and foreshadows
how reliant the community has become on interpreters today—from community
interpreting to video relay services.

I happened to be there at San Fernando Valley State College in order to
conduct classes for one week under the Institute for Secondary Teachers of the Deaf project and I was minding my own business. So what
happens? I am asked to please talk with you and given a mere two days'
notice. It did not matter that my own notes for my own classes here
have not yet jelled and need a lot of work and revamping. When one of
your instructors, Audree Norton, found out that the topic assigned to
me for the aforementioned Institute project was "Emotional Aspects of
the Deaf Adolescent," she said they couldn't have picked a better person.
I looked at her and wanted to ask just what do you mean. You know,
Audree's hands sometimes say a little but her eyes say a lot.

Okay, I am an emotional person. Anybody would be with only two
days' notice to prepare a talk for such an elite group as you interpreters. Yes, anybody would be if he had to go through what I have to go
through.

For example, if I ordered a swing set for my children or a barbecue
outfit, sure as day follows night, some part would be missing. Or, if there
was supposed to be a left and a right side I would get two left sides.
Listen to this one. A friend who was going out asked me if I would like
some ice cream.

"Yeah," I said.

"What flavor?"

The Deaf American (March 1972)

"Anything but chocolate chip."

You guessed it. I got chocolate chip.

I was asked to give my viewpoints on interpreting and interpreters. If I were asked to give a talk on total communication—no trouble. I could go on for hours.

But interpreting and interpreters! Beggars like me cannot be choosers. Interpreters are to cuddle, love and hug—the female ones, of course. Yes, I prefer female interpreters. Naturally!

To be serious, the greatest problem we deaf people have is to force our brains to cooperate with our eyes. With eyes open we can remain unseeing. What we see sometimes does not register in our minds. It is said that sound reaches the brain better than anything visual.

To be scientific, permit me to quote a passage written by Lou Fant and published in the June 1971 issue of *The Deaf American*:[10]

[. . .] Most languages of the world were meant to be spoken and heard. The ear is basically a neural organ which can accommodate the temporal quality of spoken language. The eye is neural, to be sure, but it is also a muscular organ and ill equipped to perceive the temporal quality of spoken language. The eye tires, the ear never does (though we may weary of listening, it isn't because our ears are tired). In short, vision and hearing cannot be equated, for they are separate sense modalities, the one being primarily spatial, the other temporal. Try as we might, the eye can never absorb the same amount of information as the ear, no matter how often the information is repeated.

There you have it. You must fight to get "it" across to us and we must fight to activate the muscular organ of our neural eye. Is it possible for you to approximate the temporal quality of spoken language? In other words, is it possible to approximate the cadence, the influence, the pitch of spoken language so that what is said will better register in our minds?

Never having heard for over 40 years, I am not in a position to know what cadence, inflection and pitch really are but my eyes have seen plenty—from a man lying in a pool of blood after having been hit by a car through the awakening landscape as the sun crept up to miniskirted

---

10. Lou Fant was a well-known sign language interpreter and instructor of interpreting programs.

ladies. Those interpreters who have rhythm in their arms and hands, who can rise and fall in consort with the speaker, who know when to pause and when to stress, whose face is a kaleidoscope of emotions, hold me spellbound.

I have seen interpreters whose arms and hands so resemble a whirling dervish that everything becomes a blur. On the other extreme, there have been speakers who were animated and forceful but, alas, with interpreters who came across in the same flat, dull monotone that marks the voices of some of us deaf personalities.

The most difficult to catch is the fingerspelling of words. This is understandable because the speed of the speaker causes nervousness and hurried motions so that letters jerk and do the St. Vitus dance, so that the hand turns sideways or obliquely or rotates, making it difficult to see some of the fingers. Sometimes, what are supposed to be five letters fuse and come out as only one or two.

To those of us who are postlingually deaf or who have a language base or who just want to improve ourselves, fingerspelling takes on some importance. It gives us the taste and flavor of the words used by the speaker. Depending on the topic under consideration, there are some words one would like to chew in our minds and think about its appearance in a particular place in a sentence instead of in its ideographic form.

You will have to forgive us if we become irritated when the speaker keeps on talking but the interpreter pauses seemingly leaving out large chunks of the message, when the interpreter simplifies as if we were school children, when she becomes a self-appointed censor, when there is sloppiness with hand configuration trailing off like fog under the noonday sun.

Now, I am developing guilt feelings. How dare I dwell on the few weak points in interpreting? Really, there are just a few weak points.

Interpreting today is an art more complex than it ever was in the past. What must constantly be kept in mind is that we deaf people are a motley crew. There are the prelingual, the postlingual, the oral converts, the latecomers, the mildly or severely or the in-between hard of hearing. Throw in a growing number of multiply handicapped and the emotionally disturbed who will blame you if they lose a case in court and what do you have or, rather, how do you make all of them happy? There is no way, lady. No way. But you can lessen the complaints by never keeping your lips shut. I mean always mouth the words.

We now have an atmosphere of acceptance of the language of signs never seen before. Under a benign and positive atmosphere, manual communication is crackling and expanding with seismic force. Textbooks on manual communication are proliferating and we have a constant stream of new signs being invented for technical and other usage. We have Seeing Essential English (SEE) having a California and now a Chicago version. Freed from its shackles, manual communication is now for the moment tossed and buffeted on a windy sea but it will reach port. Most Towers of Babel are short-lived.

You interpreters are special people. It is only recently that more of you are being paid for your services—and rightly so. I shudder to think of how much time and effort you have given without recompense. I like this story: An interpreter interpreted for a friend of mine all day. They went together to a party at night where my friend was the only deaf person. He moved from group to group with the interpreter but was shocked to find the interpreter not interpreting at all. After an hour or two this friend got the interpreter in a corner and said *"What's the matter with you?"* The interpreter shot back "What's the matter with you? I have my own life to live. I am here to enjoy myself." It was like a dash of cold water thrown on my friend's face but he was a man of insight, intelligence and sensitivity. It took him but a moment to see the other side.

Now, please forgive us if we do not see the other side. Please forgive us if we do not come and say "Thank you." The day is fast approaching when more of us with better education will be more attuned and sensitive to social amenities.

You have played and will play a crucial part in the new era that is here and that is gathering momentum. The new era has as its basic premise the contention that there is more to life and to living than just the acquisition of speech and speechreading skills.

Thank you, lovely people, for all you have done for us. I wish I could pick out one of you (a female, of course), fold you and put you in my wallet, taking you with me wherever I go.

The Medium Is the Message

Now that the profession of sign language interpretation has developed its own standards and practices, it is evocative to read Newman in the following speech, where he expresses candor about his own impressions of communicating with hearing people.

There are many interpretations of what Marshall McLuhan meant when he coined the phrase "The medium is the message." For my purposes this afternoon, I am going to focus on and question the medium deaf speakers use to get their messages across to an audience.

[. . .] At birthday parties, it was the custom for each child to sing a favorite song. When my turn came, my voice went something like this: "aaaAAAeeEEEawawAWAWarrrrahhhHHH." For the audience of about thirty in the room I went on for what must have been an eternity. When I stopped, everybody clapped. I felt good. I was like other children. I could sing like them.

It was not until ten years later when I began to have some sense that the whole scene hit me. I went into a cold sweat thinking how foolish I appeared, how my screams must have pierced the eardrums and almost shattered the cochleas of those who unfortunately were in attendance. When I stopped, they must have applauded wildly in relief.

When most of you were yet unborn, I was elected class valedictorian. My teacher and principal asked me to use my voice and not to sign for my valedictory address. I was told again and again, "You have good speech." I was told again and again by school people, "We can understand you."

Just before it came my turn to speak, I noticed staff members passing out sheets of paper, which turned out to be copies of my speech, to the people in the audience.

When the graduation ceremonies were over, my brother came to me and said, "I understood everything." My sense of accomplishment

Workshop, Southern California Registry of Interpreters, Los Angeles Hilton, May 6, 1978 was all too brief when a moment later a fellow graduate sided up to me and with the bluntness of youth, remarked, "My mother did not understand you at all." When I tried to say, "But . . . my brother . . . ," he quickly responded, "Why do you think the papers of your talk were passed around?"

It was a traumatic time yet a cleansing time, a time that helped me get rid of some illusions and see things as they really were.

In the last twenty years I have given hundreds of talks to various parent groups, school and college programs, clubs and organizations in many parts of our country and in Canada. When the group was small and the meeting was in a small room, I would try to use my voice. I had a way of monitoring whether or not I was understood. At the beginning, I always told a humorous anecdote or two. My eyes would sweep the audience. If there was universal laughter, I felt I was understood. In addition, I would ask or practically beg to be stopped if I were not being understood. In spite of all precautions, I will never forget the time when I was visiting lecturer on the Principles and Practices of Teaching Mathematics to the Deaf. It was a series of four lectures held on four different days. On the third day, a student came to me with excitement all over her face. "Today," she exclaimed, "I finally understood everything you said."

[. . .] But what was upsetting, more than anything else, was when a deaf speaker had a great message but delivered it in the wrong medium. It is understandable why many deaf persons choose to speak alone or to speak and sign for themselves. In one-on-one situations, they are easily understood. In restaurants and stores, no one winces when they order something. In the kingdom of the deaf, they have always been the star. Parents, teachers, relatives, friends encouraged, expected, or demanded that they use their voices turning off, by one way or another, the motor of their flying hands. On the psychological side, it was seared into them that the better they could talk, the less different and conspicuous they appeared.

An interpreter came to me and asked, "Why is it that you are realistic and ask for a reverse interpreter, while others don't?" I replied, "Have you given them feedback, and called a spade a spade?" The response I received was, "It is too touchy."

Some deaf speakers have a valid reason for wanting to speak and sign for themselves. They find that good reverse interpreters are not a dime a dozen. One deaf speaker stated that he was told his interpreter reverse interpreted in a way that made him look like a ten-year-old child. He never gave a speech again without a copy for his interpreter. Another stated that his reverse interpreter was hemming and hawing and interrupting so many times for clarification that his whole talk was ruined. There are, nevertheless, too many deaf speakers who labor under delusions of their own making or have egos that need to be brought back to earth.

I thought I could help one deaf speaker by talking to his wife. I told her, in all sincerity, that I received enough feedback to convince me that her husband was not being understood. She looked at me in a fit of impatience and retorted that her husband happened to be one of those lucky enough to have good speech and clear enough to be understood. The fact that a second interpreter had to interpret for the interpreter interpreting him apparently still did not convince her.

I feel that it is now time for my fellow deaf speakers to be told the facts of life. Perhaps they will be more aware of what actually goes on if we point out the many factors that determine whether or not the medium is effectively carrying the message.

[. . .] Deaf speakers should be aware that people who are familiar with "deaf speech" but not sign language (some parents and oral teachers, for example) may lose part of the message due to facts as:

1. The deaf speaker's volume tends to be erratic—it may start out loud enough, but lose strength later;
2. The deaf speaker's speech may be fine in one-to-one conversation but platform or stage speaking requires "fluent" speech and an appropriate rate, otherwise it becomes difficult to follow because some words may be "slurred";
3. Microphones tend to distort sound slightly, making it more difficult to understand without watching the speaker.

If there were some kind of utopia for deaf speakers to speak and sign for themselves, the following conditions would have to exist:

1. People who are familiar with deaf speech and sign language are seated in a special section.

2. Chairs in the aforementioned section have U.N.-type headsets for hearing people who want to listen to a reverse interpreter.
3. Interpreters at strategic locations throughout the audience wear headsets to receive information via reverse interpreter to translate this into Sign.
4. Monitors check the audience to be sure that all are in a state of understanding. Speaker asks for feedback every five minutes. If the audience is losing him or her, start using the reverse interpreter.

Since we do not have a utopia, should we not explore the mechanics, the different possibilities of how best to use the medium to carry the message?

It is ironic that many of us deaf people who have lived through a lifetime of communication problems often fail to understand that when we are on the platform to speak, our audience becomes handicapped. We get angry when interpreters do not fingerspell clearly, sign too rapidly, or use a ratio of one sign to five or ten spoken words. Should not we who have gone through so much frustration in communication be more sensitive to the needs of our audience? Is it not time to be realistic and not be misled by those who know us so well that they could understand us even if we spoke in Yiddish? By the same token, is it not time that those who hear us or are going to interpret for us stand tall and give it to us straight?

I am all for speech—at the right time and place. To me, the message is more important than the medium. Surely we are not on stage to strut our stuff. We are on stage to help educate and enlighten friends and strangers on what it is like to be deaf, what our experiences are, and to open our hearts and share with them our hopes and our dreams.

Float Like a Butterfly, Sting Like a Bee

The following essay holds value for future teachers of deaf students because it condenses Newman's feelings and thoughts about the appropriate modalities of communication in the classroom.

The title of this paper "Float Like a Butterfly, Sting Like a Bee," was spoken by Muhammad Ali, the former heavyweight boxing champion of the world. In what way is this relevant to the thesis of this write up? It is not in the Englishness in the elegance and telling imagery of the statement itself, yet in a way it is.

Before this contradiction confuses, let me hasten to say: the way we communicated should be unfettered; our signing hands should be able to soar or float like a butterfly or, if the occasion warrants it, come across with the sting of a bee.

It is precisely this: our hands should be unbound, not hemmed in by rules, by thou shalls and shall nots. The ultimate determinants should be: Am I clear? Do you understand me? Do I understand you? Are both the expressive and receptive parts functioning to the point that effective communication is going on?

There is so much controversy and misunderstanding in our field in the realm of communication because the points at issue are not clearly understood or fully grasped.

The first point in the form of a question is: Can language be taught? Grammar or rules of language can be taught but language itself, it would seem to me, develops with the help of some internal ticking cognitive pattern, some form of osmosis, and through a constant barrage of modeling either through human interaction or eventually the printed world.

The second point is that age is a critical factor whether one is talking about onset of deafness or the critical language input years. Before the

A Deaf American Monograph 40 (1990)

age of five, the critical factors are the establishment of an effective line of communication; otherwise there is a vacuum, a void, a wasteland. This goes a long way to explain why deafness has a devastating effect on the development of English. It should be of no surprise that when deaf children, who come from practically noncommunicating families, enter school for the first time, they do not even know their names, the names given to foods or the words to express basic daily needs. These children, perhaps however, have developed some internal language.

Surely, for them some kind of cognitive bells ring, but they have been ringing without words upon which to hang their understandings and their memories.

No wonder there is such a contrast between these children and deaf children of deaf parents or, for that matter, deaf children of effectively communicating families.

Here, we are talking about the very beginnings, the embryonic flutterings of language which is so much different when we talk about high school or college students. The expressive attempts of small, tiny hands are far different from those of bigger and more experienced hands. To these little children, the world must be a strange, multifaceted place, an array of bewildering colors and sensations. And within this context, the visual processing skills of young minds are far different from those who are older and more sophisticated.

Yes, the onset of deafness makes a big difference and it impacts on the need for different communication modes. It makes a difference if one is born deaf or became deaf later on in life . . . (in professional jargon, "the prelinguals and the postlinguals").

Other points follow:

Degree of hearing loss also makes a difference. If connected speech can be heard and understood then the person who has this function is, in most cases, way ahead in terms of language acquisition than those who were born deaf. So does the person who has enough residual hearing and can combine it with speechreading to follow the flow of speech.

Not to be ignored is the cause (etiology) of deafness. It makes a difference how one became deaf because, for example, in cases of rubella, another part of the physiognomy can be affected—the neurological cellboard, for example.

Understandable is the current furor by advocates of American Sign Language (ASL) against the inroads of systems such as Seeing Exact English (SEE), Signed English, Pidgin English (PSE), Cued Speech, etc. Understandable because history shows there was a repression of ASL which has been identified as a form of oppression of deaf people. More than that, linguists and deaf people have long felt that ASL has never been appreciated or recognized for its visual richness, its ingenuity and power, which has evolved down the years to the point where it does not waste movement or violate expressive or receptive ease. Deaf people feel ASL is part of their language and culture. This sentiment is echoed in other countries of the world.

Unfortunately, ASL has not been much used, if at all, in the homes of most families and in schools and programs for the deaf mainly during the preschool years, the critical language learning years. For deaf children with their tiny hands and still developing processing skills, it would seem that ASL would be the ideal medium of communication at this stage. Has not research already shown that, by and large, deaf children of deaf parents are way ahead in academic achievement than deaf children of hearing parents?

Not only does ASL facilitate receptive and expressive ease, it can serve as a tool to reading, to mathematics, to English itself, in fact, to a veritable storehouse of the world's knowledge. To be effective as a tool to English, for example, there must be a constant flow of association or transference from the sign to the English word or from signs to English statements and vice versa. And this, in most schools for the deaf, is what is sadly lacking.

ASL is most powerful in expressing cognitive concepts with clarity and its descriptive imagery such as in story telling.

Now, that all of this has been said and done, what then?

Reality! It stares at us with its baleful glare. How does one describe ASL? Is PSE, loosely defined as a cross between Signed English and ASL, part of ASL? Is Signed English part of ASL? Or must we lock up each in its own compartment? Are we to follow strict rules of ASL in terms of handshapes and spatial relationships? Or are we to normally follow the genesis of language?

Should not ASL be defined as a GENERIC TERM and not be compartmentalized and weighed down with rules and restrictions to the point where it does not reflect the way deaf people are actually communicating with each other in our modern society?

Surely, the languages of the world are in a constant state of flux. They have the ability to heave, shrink, expand, to spit out or swallow, adapt or adopt ASL, being a rich and flexible language in its own right, has this kind of ability.

The world of deaf people is not made up of one homogeneous group which thinks and acts the same way. It is not made up of those fed on the pap of one communication methodology. There are variations, sign dialects, borrowings, adaptations and crossovers from other systems. This comes about naturally when there are variations in onset, etiology and degree of hearing loss, not to mention geographic locations with a variety of approaches to communicating certain signs.

English itself is ever-changing. Adaptations from other languages abound. Nouns have become verbs and so on. Letters to initialize signs such as "d" in develop or "T.C." in Total Communication violates some rules of ASL but it has popular usage and should it not become part of ASL as much as "POSSLQ,"[11] which defines the current phenomenon of man and woman living together without the stamp of marriage ceremony, has become part of English idiom?

There is more to it! I mentioned age of onset, degree of hearing loss, cause of deafness, etc. We are a melting pot of all types of hearing loss. A strong case can be made for success stories in terms of English language acquisition for those who were brought up under aural/oral methods, under SEE, under Total Communication, under Cued Speech. We cannot, ostrich-like, ignore this body of evidence. But which one is the greatest good for the greatest number?

There is quite a bit of research that indicates a diversity of needs is best met under Total Communication. We can, however, pinpoint one dominant factor which is the early and effective use of communication by families in the home.

---

11. A term coined in the late 1970s by the United States Census Bureau as part of an effort to more accurately gauge the prevalence of cohabitation in American households. It is an abbreviation (or acronym) for "Persons of Opposite Sex Sharing Living Quarters," From http://en.wikipedia.org/wiki/POSSLQ.

But this is getting off the point. With so much diversity among deaf people, do we have the right to proscribe one way of communicating? For example, in a large environment such as at Gallaudet University, there is a smorgasbord of communication medleys easily explained by the fact that students come from all corners of the country with its local philosophies, sign-accents, or what-have-you. In such an environment, which approach is the greatest good for the greatest number? (By the way, a new term to replace the "old" term, simultaneous communication, has come into view. If defined in a sarcastic tone, it is Speech Supported Sign. Otherwise, it is Sign Supported Speech.)

First, let's ask how do we really use our processing skills? Globally? We look at the mouth, the face, the body, the hands? Are mouth movements not needed? Or is it easier on the eyes when there is mouth movement? And is it not true, that what we miss on the hands we catch on the lips? (The hand is faster than the eye.)

Is it not true that there is often one sign for many words and mouth movement helps us identify exactly which word the speaker is using, e.g., stop, cease, refrain? Is it not a fact that interpreters often know one sign for a variety of words that have slight gradations of meaning? On the other hand, can one really use English to teach concepts to deaf students, born deaf, profoundly deaf, who have not yet mastered this language? Would a skillful use of ASL be their saving grace? When English meets ASL, what really happens?

What about modeling and expansion? It is said one must hear a word over 30 times before it registers on the mind. When and where do modeling words and sentences and expanding on them in different ways take effect? ASL may be a powerful open sesame to reading and other subjects but deaf children—as much as hearing children need to hear it— need to see language in its living colloquial form.

We need a far more in-depth type of research to cover the questions I have posed. I suspect that such research will show that watching the hands and mouth movements together are easier on the eyes during lectures for a large number of deaf. Yet, there are these overpowering truths: ASL is attention getting like no other, easy to follow, and has no equal in getting meanings and concepts across.

Which means what? Reality, again! It would be naïve to suppose that many non deaf people will be able to overcome motoric dysfunction and use ASL. A strict screening out of those unable to use ASL would leave us on an island unto ourselves. And this is in light of the growing shortage of special education teachers.

Not to be ignored are the parents who have an overwhelming desire for their children to learn to talk and use residual hearing. I would like to see more of a bilingual approach of the type used by Tripod at Burbank, California,[12] where both a deaf and hearing teacher are in the same classroom with deaf tots.

I am sure that we all agree that the ultimate goal for deaf children is the acquisition and mastery of the English language so that they can pass tests in English, read and write directions, become aware of and do commerce with his or her world, savor tales and harrowing experiences in the world of books, and so on.

Blessed is he or she who can shift from one mode to another, modeling and expanding when needed, bringing the richness and elegance of English across to young minds and using much of one of the Seven Wonders of the World, ASL, to draw out thinking and to get across concepts, ideas and knowledge in a powerful way.

In the meantime, our hands should be able to float like a butterfly or sting like a bee.

Otherwise, we will begin to s-s-s-st-stu-ter-ter.

---

12. The Tripod Educational Model School, an educational program that has since become part of the Burbank Unified School District. providing a model for "reverse mainstreaming." Services are offered via a center-program like model, from parent/infant through elementary school.

Part Three

ON PARENTING DEAF CHILDREN — COMMUNICATION, EDUCATION, RELATIONSHIPS, AND EXPERIENCES

Newman says of Betty, his wife: "It was a marriage made in heaven. She is the sweetest, most patient woman I have ever known. She has put up with me and brought up my five children, all while teaching full time. She has had to deal with high blood pressure. She was always extremely busy. She kept the children neat and well-fed. She took care of the house when I was off on my speaking trips or working a long distance away at Taft, teaching at night, etc."

The Newmans had five children. The first four children were hearing, and Carol, an unexpected child, turned out to be deaf. The experience of being a parent to a deaf child proved too valuable of an opportunity for a writer like Newman to pass up.

Cherry Blossoms Come to Bloom

Here, Newman uses his extensive experiences as a teacher and a father of a deaf daughter to reflect on the challenges facing parents of deaf children. He uses humor in his writings and talks to parents to further his cause, and always pushes the case for what has now become known as early intervention. Some of his writings and talks can be seen as a training guide in honesty and tact for administrators and teachers of deaf children. His philosophy can be summed up in a line that he wrote in a column in The Deaf American: "The best gift you can give your deaf child is the gift of yourself."

We were totally unprepared for our deaf daughter, Carol Lee. Already in our forties and already having brought up four other hearing children, we had enough of diapers and pabulum.

Carol Lee has more than a 95% decibel hearing loss. She is now a little over three years of age and, as we gaze fondly at her, we both agree she is the most beautiful mistake we ever made. Some people cannot stop eating potato chips. We cannot stop kissing her.

The greatest predicament that faces parents of deaf children is now how to help the child talk and speechread and use auditory aids. In the hands of parents is a deaf child whose mind is a veritable *tabula rasa*. What do they do with a deaf child without language, without the means to receive and convey thoughts in the normal way? How can their deaf child be helped to learn language and thus become tuned in and responsive to the world of the hearing?

Aware that thought comes before language, that the wheels in the mind must turn so that there will be readiness for learning, we placed mobile units over our daughter's playpen. Moving plastic birds and butterflies attract an infant's eyes. Next came learning toys based on graduation of size and matching of different shapes. Carol would rather play with puzzles than with dolls. We had difficulty at first but finally we were permitted to enroll her in a branch of the International Montessori Schools where a large part of learning was based on non-verbal tasks.

The Deaf American (July–August 1972)

It seems logical that a child's mind be stimulated by non-verbal tasks as early as possible so that there will be recognition, perception, and the development of skills to perceive patterns between relationships and associations. This kind of development helps speechreading and all forms of learning. It creates the conditions for thinking and for an awareness of what people are saying and doing.

A prelingual deaf child must have a symbol system that is visually oriented and that is almost tangible so that she will have a means of expressing herself, of understanding what her parents are talking about and for storing in her memory identifications of familiar objects and incidents that have occurred. It is almost impossible for a prelingual deaf child of two years of age to speak or speechread "squirrel" or "crocodile" but it is possible to sign them or recognize the signs for them at an age earlier than two.

When we changed Carol Lee's diapers we made the signs for *mommy, daddy, love, you wet?* Here was gross movement and three-dimensional appearance in space that a deaf infant's eyes will follow, will learn to distinguish, and to associate with something relevant. No other communication method in the world can equal hand signs in its richness, ingenuity, grace, and flexibility. Daily, we brought to our child a live Sesame Street.

A baby has immediate needs—to be cuddled and fed and, if it can hear, to be spoken to. If the baby cannot hear, common sense dictates that we do more than just mouth words, more than just hope that the hearing aid will take care of everything.

Holding our Carol near a campfire we both vocalized and signed the world for "hot." There was no response but two weeks later, back home from a vacation trip, she put her hand on our clothes dryer and made the sign for "hot."

Input is the first stage. Parents and educators often expect immediate output or performance and if this does not occur they think they have not reached the child or have failed which, of course, is not true. After two months of input our daughter at 10 months of age made the sign for *daddy* but this was the same sign for *mommy*. It took two more months of input before she could make a different sign for *mommy* and *daddy*.

If we had vocalized alone could we have succeeded as well? There is no doubt in our minds that we could not because moving hands are attention-getting for children whose ages are measured in months. We deaf people place extra burdens on our eyes to clue us in on what goes on around us. Our eyes are constantly searching for clues or hints or revealing motions other people make. Lip movements are the smallest in the animated category, the most ambiguous and the most difficult to follow in the communication process. If this is true for deaf adults, how much more so for babies and young children.

We might be told that many deaf children are progressing under the oral method alone. The fact remains that no one has bothered to document the depth and quality of the progress. There is a difference between a parroting and a communicating personality. An audiologist friend of mine wrote to three different preschool oral programs asking for progress reports of their two-, three-, and four-year-old children. She received no reply from any one of them. I happen to know that one of the three schools uses the same few children over and over again for demonstration purposes.

From 16 to 22 months of age Carol's single word sign production grew rapidly to 60 words. Of course, she quickly learned the signs for *candy, cookie, ice cream*. She also had signs for *dog, cat, wrong, right, pretty, more, dirty* and for two-word combinations such as *daddy work, cookie eat, me funny, boy laughing*. She could tell us which drink she wanted—water, milk, soda pop or orange juice. When I asked hearing parents of deaf children how they knew which drink their child wanted I was told "by pointing."

What is intriguing is the way Carol uses the same sign in a spiral form as she grows older and becomes more aware of subtle shades of meanings. "More cookie" becomes "Pull up socks more." It has been fascinating to watch her expressions expand from single to two, three and now several word sentence statements such as "Me swim, sleep, wake up, eat cookie cookie." Recently, with mouth imitating the whir of an airplane, she said "Father fly finish, come Sunday."

Dr. Ursula Bellugi and Dr. Edward S. Klima have been making videotape records and studying the language development of deaf children of deaf parents (including our Carol) at the Salk Institute, La Jolla, Calif. In their article "The Roots of Language in the Sign Talk of the Deaf" printed in the June 1972 issue of *Psychology Today*, they state that in their study of one of the children, Pola, they find that in her early combination of signs is "the full range of semantic relations expressed by hearing children." They go on to state that "It does seem that, in spite of the change in modality, the milestones of language development may be the same." They make note of the fact that "The vocabulary of sign language makes many more discriminations about ways of looking and seeing than spoken English does."[1]

To have a sense of perspective we need to compare the progress of a deaf child with that of a hearing child. A hearing child at the age of 18 months has a 25-word vocabulary while a deaf child customarily has no vocabulary, no understanding. A hearing child at the age of 2–3 years understands directions, uses short sentences, asks questions, relates experience, understands adults well and has a 500-word vocabulary while a deaf child has a vocabulary of a few words, and yells or screeches to express desires and wants.[2]

Each sibling in our family is identified by Carol by the first letter of his or her name. For example, she forms the letter "R" with her fingers and shakes it if she intends it to stand for her sister, Rochelle. Bojo, our dog, was abbreviated to BJ. She became curious and began to finger-spell other letters. Soon she was fingerspelling such words as: *off, ok, no, jump, hole, oh*. At one time she broke a drinking glass. I scolded her and told her to be careful. She fingerspelled back "ok." At another time, the tables were turned, and I broke two bottles of soda. She signed "Be careful" and I fingerspelled "ok." She would fingerspell words from books, newspapers or even from the walls of toilets. Surely, the foundation for reading readiness is being laid.

Deaf students have difficulty understanding the abstract. We taught Carol the sign for "flower" and added the sign for "beautiful." When she received a new blue coat with a furry collar, she exclaimed in sign "beautiful." Her ability to use on her own power an abstract notion in a different context is, I think, unusual for a deaf child of her age.

Because we established an effective line of communication with our daughter, we think, we have laid the groundwork for good physical, emotional and mental health. We can reason with her: "Eat first, candy later." How many times, in frustration, have parents and others in our field slapped deaf children unnecessarily or without any explanations?

---

1. Ursula Bellugi and Edward S. Klima, "The Roots of Language in the Sign Talk of the Deaf," *Psychology Today* (June 1972): 61–76.

2. James A. Little, ed., *Answer* (Santa Fe: New Mexico School for the Deaf, 1970): 20–22.

When Carol was ill she was able to use the sign for "hurt" near her ear or her stomach to tell us exactly what was bothering her. At one time, as I was leaving her room, she made the sign for "leave." Frozen in my tracks, I tried to figure out what she meant. It soon dawned on me that she wanted me to "leave" the lights on. She was not even two years old and she could tell us she was not reluctant to go to sleep but just did not want to be left alone in the dark.

How does a parent make sure a deaf child understands that something is dangerous and can cause injury? We discussed with Carol what would happen if one is hit by a car and, therefore, how important it was to look both ways before crossing the street. In no time we caught her walking to the edge of a sidewalk. She stopped and signed to herself "Look both ways" then she crossed her arms, rested them on her chest and looked up and down the street several times before crossing.

At a little past the age of three, Carol has a vocabulary of around 300 words and can string out sentences manually in crude but meaningful ways. But this does not tell the whole story—far from it.

Like cherry blossoms come to bloom, the best and most important part is the flowering of her mind. Because she was given an effective visual and expressive symbol system she has been able to recall past events—the animals visited at the zoo, the Railroader, a restaurant where we all ate together, the visit to her grandparents. An internal language structure seems to be developing within her rather than being superimposed upon her by drills and imitation. She is able to manipulate her thoughts into expressions that make sense. She gave me a piece of gum and when I greedily asked for another one, she said "You pig, fat you pig." Coming from a deaf child, it seems like a miracle, like a soul set free to communicate joyously.

Our daughter enjoys herself and takes pleasure in herself. She is free to use her hands or to use her voice. She will sign to the ocean waves saying "Stay, stay" as they creep near her mudpies. She will talk to herself or to her dog, urging him to eat. She will yell at her daddy with her hands saying "bad, bad, bad," if he drives away without taking her. She was toilet trained before the age of two. Because there was reciprocal communication we could tease each other and when she entered preschool her sense of humor showed.

Both my wife and I are teachers but we kept formal teaching to a minimum because we are aware of the importance of being parents first. We kept communication spontaneous, natural and fun. First, we used Ameslan, then a little fingerspelling any time she was in a receptive mood, and as our daughter moved through different levels of readiness, we added the new signs in current use such as the signs that distinguish bus, car, truck and those for verb tenses and verb endings. There was no need to be extreme in any one system or method but to try to meet her communication needs as the months went by.

With our daughter we followed the philosophy of total communication. We did not force her but gradually led her to the wearing of a hearing aid even though she had more than 90% decibel loss. Once a week she has a one hour session with an audiologist in addition to the part-time oral-aural methods utilized in her total communication preschool class. Her teacher, who received her training at the Central Institute for the Deaf, stated that Carol could speechread in one month what ordinarily it took other deaf children a whole school year to become that proficient. She also mentioned that Carol forms and speaks many words normally.

At home we would encourage her to talk and we would talk to her without signing to give her practice in speechreading. We seldom made any formal attempts to teach her such skills but allowed them to develop in a natural way. Because her mind was stimulated at an early age, she became aware of what others were doing and saying and thus was receptive to learning. In preschool she is now being taught speech elements that are not visible on the lips.

This question comes to mind: At what point in time should a deaf child be formally taught speech? Should not an effective line of communication first be established under the umbrella of total communication? Should not pains first be taken to see that there is a stimulating environment so that the gears in a deaf child's mind will mesh and he or she can become a spontaneously communicating and responsive individual? When proper child development sequences are followed will there then be more readiness and receptiveness for oral-aural methods? Have the people in our field missed the boat by insisting upon and forcing oral-aural methods alone, at the wrong time and for too prolonged a duration? Here lies the crux of the matter. Why have not more thorough scientific research undertakings been brought to bear on this?

Dr. Hilda Schlesinger in her research study *Deafness and Mental Health: The Developmental Years*[3] stated that little attention has been paid to the motoric-speech relationship. What is it, for example, that causes hearing babies to wave their hands when they say "bye-bye"? She made a clinical study of four families with deaf children—two pairs of hearing parents and two pairs of deaf parents—and she found that when manual communication was used early the deaf children began to use their speech more and signs less. Dr. Schlesinger stated that if parents accepted the child's preferred mode of communication the child will use other methods through association pathways. This is the direct antithesis of what is presented to parents—"If you let your child use his hands he will not learn to talk."

It is interesting to note that in Dr. Schlesinger's research on 40 preschool children she found that more than 50% of parents complained about frustration involving understanding—15% could not understand child and 38% could not be understood by child. The percentage increased as the child grew older.[4]

Professionals in our field tell us that one reason deaf children of deaf parents are ahead of deaf children of hearing parents is because the children are accepted quickly while hearing parents go through traumatic stages of guilt feelings, despair, then the search for remedies or means that will somehow minimize their child's hearing loss or restore him or her to society. How true this is is open to question but this serves to divert parents from the basic cause of what is wrong in many aspects of the field of education of the deaf. Once parents can get at the basic cause there is no reason why the initial shock cannot be overcome and hearing parents do as well as deaf parents, if not better.

The basic cause is the lack of effective communication in the home during the critical first few years of the deaf child's life. The rejection of one of the communication modalities—manual communication that is used by almost all deaf people—is a contributing factor. As Dr. Bellugi and Dr. Klima state:

---

3. H. Schlesinger and K. Meadow, "Deafness and Mental Health: A Developmental Approach," in *Deafness and Mental Health: The Developmental Years* (San Francisco: Langley Porter Neuropsychiatric Institute, 1971): 163–164.

4. Schlesinger and Meadow, "Deafness and Mental Health," p. 169.

Sign Language, it is clear, is far more than mystical hand-waving. Its range and diversity permit humor and pun, song and poetry, whimsy and whispering. What it lacks in comparison with spoken English it amply compensates for in other ways. The study of sign language gives us insight into the structure of language and the universality of communication, but even more it attests to the richness of human intelligence and imagination.[5]

I suspect that even after counseling, attendance at preschool clinics, association with others in similar circumstances, too many parents feel inadequate or unable to cope with their deaf offspring. Basically, this is a result of insufficient information parents receive. They are not made aware of alternatives or options if one method of communication is found to be inadequate.

What is needed are training centers for parents of deaf children that show how total communication can be used effectively in the home. With a shelf full of communication tools at their disposal, parents will be in a better position to select one or change from one to another according to the varying needs at differing age levels of their children.

We can no longer be satisfied if a deaf child knows a few words or can speak a few words. He has the same normal intelligence as a hearing child and there is no reason for him or her to be too far behind in reading and language skills. We should zero in on the deaf child who is from one to five years of age and study his progress. In fact, if most of our time and energies and if most of the research studies were devoted to this critical age we will be seeing the light at the end of the tunnel.

---

5. Bellugi and Klima, "The Roots of Language," 76.

Can You Hear It, My Daughter?

Does a waterfall make a sound
Or snowflakes landing on the ground?
Can you hear it, my daughter
The splashing of the water
Snowflakes and falling leaves in flight
Are the sounds the same or none at all?
Nature is there for your delight.
Or would you rather ignore its call?
The flapping of the robin's wings
Wonder how it sounds as it sings?
While you play and have your fun
Can you hear my footsteps as I run
And come behind you. The surprise
That lights your eyes tells me otherwise.
Do not worry, dearest girl of ours
Go and pick and smell the flowers
Let your eyes look to the stars
Let your thoughts weave moonbeams
They help you around most snares
They help you fulfill your dreams
But this above them all—come winter snow
Spring chill, summer winds or leafy show
Of fall—you can be sure
Our love will always endure:
As long as your siblings are there,
As long as your mom and dad are here . . .

Girl with a Whirligig

Thrust, thrust your stick up high
And wait for the wind to blow
Little girl with whirligig.
Watch your world go round
In folds of angular convergence.

Stroll the sidewalks of your innocence
Clutching fingers of security.
Around the corner is your womanhood
That cannot wait for the wind to blow,
Little girl with whirligig.

What dreams, what trips are taken
Within the torrents of the mind?
Can a whirligig be your heirloom?
No . . .
And yet we know—or do we really—
In the darkness of the evening
A firefly glows.

Social Education (May 1969)

The Best Gift —
The Gift of Yourself

Following is an excerpt from a newspaper article telling of a "Show and Tell" reading session with hearing kindergarten children:

> Angie had been to Fairmount Park where she and her family had a whole bunch of fun and she got to drive the boat and then mama said, "Oh, it's cold" and they rode on the roller coaster and saw a helicopter.
>
> The children were listening and some were asked to recite. There was work with words grouped for similar sounds: Ben, men: Dan, man; tan, tam: a man in a tan tam. The meaning of an exclamation point was explained in stride: "You say that with lots of feeling. 'That Big Cat!'"

The vast flow of language being assimilated by those hearing children stands in stark contrast to the pitiful amount to which deaf children are being exposed.

In another incident, a three-year-old hearing boy shouted: "Give me a shove, grandma." I decided to ask my class of bright, alert 17- to 19-year-old deaf students what "give me a shove" meant. Not one of them knew.

There would be extreme difficulty in trying to explain the meaning of an exclamation point to deaf children of kindergarten age. For these children, words grouped for similar sounds remain unheard. So are words that define some of their daily experiences. So deleterious are the effects of deafness that it is commonplace for deaf children, 16 years of age or older, to copy words on paper laboriously letter by letter instead of in a natural sweeping manner.

Many words appear as familiar to deaf students as they do to hearing students studying a foreign language for the first time. When the word "beware" was written on the blackboard with the first letter not too legible, I would be asked by student after student if it were spelled "feware." Few deaf students can recognize, let alone understand, such familiar

---

The Deaf American (April 1969)

sayings as: "Business is business." "The black sheep in the family." "She let the cat out of the bag." Many deaf persons of average intelligence, even the ones who are avid sports spectators or participants, do not know the meaning of "penalty," "goal," "attaboy."

These are but bits and shreds of a wealth of evidence that vividly shows how much the deaf are cut off from a world of words, phrases, familiar statements and sayings. They accentuate how great has been the failure to have them become familiar with the printed word.

Books, a powerful factor in the mental development of mankind, should be the saving grace for the majority of deaf persons but they are not.[6] There is no question but that deaf children, like their hearing counterparts, can be read to and that they have a keen appetite for stories. Could the failure to feed this appetite be traced to communication restrictions in schools for the deaf? To a failure to inform and educate parents of the fact that there are flexible methods of communicating with their deaf children? Why has there been a failure to publicize to an extensive manner Mr. Hofsteater's story of how his deaf parents taught him to read?[7] The interest and curiosity of children are aroused when stories are dramatized. It is doubtful if any other group of people have in them the ability—to bring stories dramatically alive as do those who are skillful in manual communication. It would be a revelation to witness deaf children being enthralled by such master storytellers. They go through the same emotional catharsis as, say, an audience held spellbound by the moving cadences of a voice singing "Under the Shadow of Your Smile."

But dramatizing stories is not enough. Perhaps many parents do not realize it but they can play an important role in the educational growth of their deaf children. There is nothing better than they can do for them than to develop in them a love for reading. The task is prodigious but so are the rewards. I have seen with my own eyes the ungrammatical language of two of my deaf friends transformed into smooth, natural

---

6. Here, Newman points out that reading is the most common way to model the English language, but deaf students do not generally read books.

7. A reference to an article by Mr. Howard Hofsteater that appeared in *The Silent Worker* in June 1950. His parents taught him to read by associating the manual and print alphabet with symbols.

language, into the writing of poetry. It occurred over a period of five years with the help of daily doses of reading.

Exactly what can parents do? They can create a stimulating environment in such a way that the deaf child actually undergoes some of the experiences depicted in stories such as going to the zoo or visiting a museum. A line of communication must be established so that the deaf child can understand a concept and relate it to what he is reading. It is the breakdown in communication that contributes to frustration and to retreat. If this is the case, then parents must seek out and learn a more flexible means of communication—speech, speechreading, fingerspelling, signs, used in combination or simultaneously for maximum results. Lucky the deaf child whose parents are born hams, whose parents realize that their role is a crucial factor that can make a lifelong difference in a child's attitude toward future education.

Too often the verbal content but not the subject matter of "Little Red Riding Hood" is suitable for the deaf. Care, therefore, must be invested in the proper selection of books for your deaf child. Start with a picture dictionary and picture stories. Look up the literature on reading. For example, there were reprints of "Books of High Interest and Low Vocabulary level to Meet the Needs of Deaf Students in Grades Seven Through Twelve" from the September 1946 issue of the *American Annals of the Deaf*, prepared by Laura Lange Crosby.[8]

Most parents already have large amounts of patience, love and understanding and the knowledge that children are not made up of just sugar and spice, snails and puppy-dogs' tails but also of thirsty minds waiting to be transformed to faraway places, waiting to be stirred by Lochinvar,[9] Hamlet, Longfellow, waiting to understand the world around them.

Please do not let them wait in vain. The best gift you can give your deaf child is the gift of yourself.

---

8. Laura Lange Crosby, "Books of High Interest and Low Vocabulary level to Meet the Needs of Deaf Students in Grades Seven Through Twelve" *American Annals of the Deaf 93*, no. 4 (September 1948): 339–59.

9. A young Scottish hero that is the subject of *Marmion*, an epic poem by Sir Walter Scott.

A Talk Before Parents

O n seven different occasions this year I have been invited to talk to various groups, mostly to parents of deaf children. The following talk was delivered at a PTCA panel meeting at the California School for the Deaf, Riverside:

Anyone who was associated with me, after I became deaf at the age of five from mastoiditis, would have thought that Dennis the Menace was an angel. I took out my frustrations at being deaf by thrusting my first through a pane of glass, by shooing customers out of my father's bakery, by sitting on a wedding cake he had just made, and by bullying weaker members of my class at the Lexington School for the Deaf located in New York City. An older deaf person at this school described me as a chicken still jumping around after its head had been chopped off. She meant I was jumping around, talking to anyone in sight, acting as if I still could hear.

Even a child soon learns the hard realities of life. Home from school, I tried to act just like any other kid, but I soon found out that talking to and trying to understand what others were saying were two different things. Children and adolescents are not as patient or understanding as adults (at least, some adults) and I soon found myself with a brand new basketball in my hands and no one to play with.

Human beings are a highly adaptable species (except when they appear in divorce court) and since we deaf belonged to the human race we learned that the best thing to do was to spend a weekend at a deaf friend's house—of the same sex, of course.

My parents and two brothers were all heart, smothering me in love. They never laid a finger on me (my wife sometimes wishes it were otherwise) even when I sat on that wedding cake. My parents would repeat a word 10 times before I finally understood. It often left us emotionally exhausted and, without thinking of it or meaning to, the framework of communication within which we moved tended to be restricted to such

The Deaf American (May 1969)

essentials as: It is time to eat; we are going out and will be back, be good, etc. A visit to relatives involved group dynamics that left a deaf person out in the cold. When I asked what they were talking about, "Nothing important," was their answer. I soon learned to curl myself up in a corner with a book.

One of my brothers could fingerspell a little and he would tell me in a few words what a two-hour movie was all about. I would attend theatres where foreign films were being shown because they had English captions but the women in those films were often undressing and it was difficult to keep my eyes on them and the captions at the same time. Now that American films are being captioned for the deaf I do not understand how, in my salad days, I ever sat still for three or four hours at a movie house.

Let me tell you what deafness is. Deafness is continuing to use the vacuum cleaner when the plug has been jerked out of its socket: being singled out for a chat by talkative persons although there are hundreds around you who can hear: nodding, making faces, and pretending you understand instead of telling the person he might as well be talking in Swahili; smiling when the person is telling you about his wife who has just died and contorting your face into a sad expression when you are told the funniest joke known to man.

Deafness is wondering if the persons over there are talking about you and laughing at you; wondering what you would do if you were in a bank at the exact moment it was being robbed by those wearing face masks not exactly conducive to lipreading.

Son Warner, brother Lenny, son-in-law Sandy.

Deafness is, if you are prelingually deaf, not knowing the meaning of such common words as "Attaboy," "Beware"; not being familiar with a prehippie era saying such as: "As American as apple pie"; not being able to write a grammatically correct sentence; having minds dulled by years of communication starvation.

Deafness is thanking God for sensible parents who send their deaf children to schools where a flexible method of communication is employed yet wondering why some of our own families are more worried about our speech and lipreading abilities than our reading, writing and reasoning skills; wondering why our families want us to spend 15 years learning speech and lipreading while some of them do not put in at least one hour to learn fingerspelling; wondering why our own families seldom tell us stories, a joke, a full hour's interpretation of a television program or make us part of the dinner-table conversation.

How many realize the actual education status of the deaf on a national level? How many realize that deaf children of deaf parents show superior academic achievement compared to deaf children of hearing parents and, surprisingly, have as good speech? Please let me show you a few research findings, documented by McCay Vernon in his article "Social and Psychological Factors in Profound Hearing Loss," *Journal of Speech and Hearing Research*.[10]

In one study it was shown that of the 93 percent of deaf students in the United States age 16 years or older:

30 percent were functionally illiterate;
60 percent had a grade level 5.3 or below;
Only 5 percent achieved a tenth grade achievement test score or better (most were postlingually deaf or hard of hearing).

In another study of 73 school programs representing 54 percent of deaf school children ages 10 to 16:

1. Average gain in reading from age 10 to 16 was less than one year (0.8 month)
2. Average reading achievement of 16-year-olds was grade level 3.4

---

10. This article appeared in the September 1969 issue of *Journal of Speech and Hearing Research* 12: 541–563.

3. 80 percent of 16-year-olds were below grade level 4.9 in reading
4. 1.7 percent of deaf school age population attend colleges for the deaf
   compared to 9.7 percent of hearing school age population

Five research studies were made by Stuckless and Birch (1966),[11] Montgomery (1966),[12] Meadow (1967),[13] Stevenson (1964),[14] and Quigley and Frisina (1961)[15] on deaf children of deaf parents and deaf children of hearing parents.

All except one showed that deaf children of deaf parents had as good speech as deaf children of hearing parents, were better lipreaders, were better in reading and writing. 38 percent of deaf children of deaf parents went to college versus 9 percent of the other group. At the California School for the Deaf, Riverside, the average IQ of deaf children of deaf parents was 113. Of deaf children of hearing parents it was 104. This is *statistically significant*.

These research findings are both gloomy and hopeful. In the case of deaf children of deaf parents we have strong clues that the type of communication carried on at their homes should be duplicated to some extent in the formal setting of the classroom. In some places we are moving in the right direction. If you will pardon my chauvinism, here at CSDR we have children as young as five years of age carrying on communication in a more relaxed and flexible manner. More important, we have people in authority who are open-minded about trying out different approaches.

In closing, I would like to say that living, feeding and clothing us do not seem to be enough. Our souls need to be reached and our awareness

---

11. E. R. Stuckless and J. W. Birch, "The Influence of Early Manual Communication on the Linguistic Development of Deaf Children," *American Annals of the Deaf* 111, no. 4 (1966): 452–504.

12. G. W. G. Montgomery, "The Relationship of Oral Skills to Manual Communication in Profoundly Deaf Adolescents," *American Annals of the Deaf* 111, no. 4 (1966): 557–565.

13. K. P. Meadow, "The Effect of Early Manual Communication and Family Climate on the Deaf Child's Development" (Unpublished PhD, University of California, Berkeley, 1967).

14. E. A. Stevenson, *A Study of the Educational Achievements of Deaf Children of Deaf Parents* (Berkeley: California School for the Deaf, 1964).

15. S. Quigley and R. Frisina, *Institutionalization and Psychoeducational Development of Deaf Children*, CEC Research Monograph (Washington, DC: Council on Exceptional Children, 1961).

of the world in which we live developed. We have never asked that you remove your glasses, put cotton in your ears and see and hear the hard way, but we do ask that more of you learn to communicate with us flexibly and spontaneously. There is no greater way to help us realize our potential, no greater way to show your understanding, your love, and the fact that living can be joyful.

Panel Talk — Viewpoints of a Deaf Teacher of the Deaf, Sacramento — May 2, 1970

Upon being a parent, Newman became involved with local and national parent organizations, eventually becoming the president of the International Association of Parents of the Deaf (IAPD), now the American Society for Deaf Children (ASDC). The following talks are proof that while Newman was a seasoned educator of the deaf, he was also venturing into the unknown as the parent of a deaf child. His empathy for his own child and determination that she would succeed spilled over to every other deaf child that he encountered.

When I was on a plane trip to Washington, DC, several months ago, the movie *Gambit* starring Michael Caine and Shirley MacLaine was shown. The movie had some action and it seemed interesting but for the life of me, I could not tell what it was all about. Like a jigsaw puzzle, many pieces were missing. Then a few weeks ago I saw this film again, this time, with English captions. The pieces fell into place and I enjoyed the movie thoroughly. I might have missed out on background sounds, the inflection and tenor of the actors' voices but who was I to complain. After 25 years of sitting in movie houses trying to understand the plot and action and pretending that I did, there now is effective communication. I found myself thinking of the clever way words were used by the film characters in their conversations. I felt mentally stimulated.

The daily vicissitudes of life that face us deaf adults is akin to a movie film without captions—that is, there is little or no effective communication. Two aspects of communication should be noted here—the receptive and the expressive. The receptive involves lipreading and the expressive speech. They are two birds of a different feather. Although there are some deaf persons who are good in both, it does not automatically

---

The Deaf American (June 1970)

follow that if a deaf person is good in the receptive part he is also good in the expressive part, or vice versa.

When it comes to the receptive part of communication, there is often a feeling of uncertainty. The nagging question is in the back of our heads—will the person be as easy to lipread as some of our teachers and relatives? Will speech come from a mouth opened just a teeny weensy bit? Some lips are made, believe me, more for kissing than for lipreading.

Both the receptive and expressive aspects came into play when at a travel agency I wrote down my travel plans. The agent communicated back to me by writing. Then I forgot myself and talked to him. Immediately, he talked back, beard and all, as if I were a hearing person. Not wanting to land in Timbuctoo I insisted he stick to writing.

In all the years people have talked to me there were but a few I could lipread without tension and uncertainty—so rare were they that they were like an oasis in the desert. What happens is that I try to anticipate, guess, follow logical possibility or just nod my head in what I hope is the correct direction.

The type of mouth movement, the physical shape of teeth and lips are but part of the factors involved in lipreading. Compounding the problem is the fact that "40 to 60% or more of the sounds of English are homophenous, that is, they look like some other sound on the lip . . ."[16] One study showed that the best speechreaders in a one-to-one situation understood only 26% of what is said while many bright otherwise capable deaf children grasped less than 5%.[17]

When it comes to the expressive part, I often find that instead of ordering Fresca I order a Coke because it is easier to say, because the chances are less of being misunderstood. I like pistachio ice cream but vanilla is easier for me to say so I order this and what happens? I get the last flavor I want—banana. I try to remember that banquet is not pronounced bang-kay but bang-kwet while bouquet is not pronounced boh-kwet but boh-kay. On top of the extra things we have to do, we have to memorize accent, pronunciation and, if we can, inflection.

The yearning and need of the deaf to communicate without having to face receptive and expressive problems are great. Wherever they

---

16. Vernon, "Sociological and Psychological Factors," p. 541–563.
17. Ibid.

congregate—at presentation of plays or skits or at sports events—they chat with each other way past closing time. It is as if they were trying to make up for lost time.

Now, let us focus on deaf students. Other than the way he speaks, what marks a deaf student more than anything else is his limited ability to verbalize and read. English, for all intents and purposes, is practically a foreign language to them. Even their word recognition is so poor that such words as "printed" and "painted" blur and fuse until to the eyes of some of the deaf they become one and the same thing. They do not comprehend simple words which we take for granted, words such as "anxious," "comment" and so on. Their misspelling of words reaches dimensions of unreality: liability becomes linbarrity. Notice that here we do not have words misspelled because of the way they sound.

Less noticed and mentioned is the short memory span of an increasing number of students who cannot recall what was taught a day or even a few minutes ago. Perhaps this has become more pronounced because of the increasing number of prelingual deaf now in schools for the deaf. In fact, 95% became deaf before they had a chance to form a language base.[18]

The attention span of the deaf is also limited. The teacher must constantly make sure the student is alert and concentrating. It is not uncommon for a student's eyes to be upon you but for his mind to be far away.

Now then, the fact that [many] deaf[19] do not have [English] language and reading abilities, the fact that they have short memory and attention spans become understandable in light of the type of communication they have had at home and during their early years in school—"communication without captions." We should not be surprised—but disturbed, yes. After all, fifty investigations have shown that deaf people "as a group have essentially the same intelligence as the non-deaf."[20]

Let us go back to the movie that I saw—the one without captions. Throughout the movie I caught only a handful of words on the lips of the film stars. I remember catching Michael Caine saying "five thousand dollars" but a fat lot of good it did me. As the dialogue continued I found myself occasionally indulging in reverie.

---

18. Vernon, "Social and Psychological Factors."

19. Newman means that for most deaf people, the gap between English and sign language is greater than perceived.

20. *The Deaf American* (March 1970): 13.

For hearing children communication usually is instantaneous and sure while unlike them, deaf children must strain and struggle to make sense out of what people are saying. For example, they must first identify and then comprehend what they see on the lips. It is strange, but few persons have ever questioned how and what in the world deaf children can lipread if they do not have the vocabulary and the language in the first place. Because of unreasonable demands made on them, they will retreat into themselves and indulge in reverie or they will nod their heads, like we deaf adults continue to do, and pretend that they understand.

All their young lives deaf children, like myself at the movie, have caught a word here and there. They have learned to repeat some words orally. Everyone is proud of them if they learn to speak and read on the lips a "fish," a "top," a "shoe." Yet the fact is that "teaching a deaf child the speech for a particular word does not in any way guarantee that the child knows the language or the meaning of the word."[21] And what he lipreads is not correct grammatical language flow. When one considers the fact that hearing children at the age of four have a vocabulary of 4,000 compared to 20 for the deaf and that they can follow the rules of grammar and syntax to combine these words in many meaningful ways,[22] one can see that the problems involved in educating the deaf are monumental.

It is important that one understands the difference between a one-to-one communication situation and that of a one-to-six or more. For example, the angle of view, the play of light and shadow all change. A deaf child might be able to converse with a parent orally to a certain extent but this does not mean he will be able to follow classroom communication. Good classroom dynamics mean that children themselves participate and communicate. It is considered a poor method when the teacher dominates the classroom activities and tells the children what to do too often. Now, Billy with teeth braces will not be easy to lipread. Jean might not feel free to express herself. Tom might happen to be the type that just cannot lipread much.

Before I continue I would like to emphasize that we deaf people consider the ability to speak and lipread priceless assets. We would be among the first to protest if schools did not continue to use and teach them. We

---

21. R. A. Brill, presentation, Maryland State Department of Education.
22. Ibid.

consider amplification and auditory training a fine thing for those who can benefit. It should be emphasized, however, that "because there is sound perception it does not necessarily follow that connected speech is understood."[23] Speech, lipreading, amplification and auditory training are subsidiary parts of communication, that is, they are not communication itself. We protest when they are not treated as just a part in the total development of the deaf as thinking human beings, when manual communication is excluded.

If there were a formal acceptance and use of manual communication both at home and in the classroom in addition to speech and lipreading there would be for us deaf people "communication with captions." With the help of just two hands we deaf people have been able to recite poetry, act in plays, and communicate anything to each other. Manual communication should be considered one of the Seven Wonders of the World but it has been unjustifiably made the scapegoat for some of our shortcomings and it has never been accepted by those, who after all, do not need to use it.

To many parents, manual communication poses a threat. There is the fear that if allowed to use their hands deaf children will not want to learn to talk and lipread and they will not have the necessary practice and development of skills. The assertion is often made that the deaf must learn to live in a hearing world. On the surface the logic seems persuasive but what are the facts?

We have long suspected that deaf children of deaf parents were more alert and knowledgeable, more aware of what was going on. Of five research studies made on deaf children of deaf parents and deaf children of hearing parents, all except one showed that deaf children of deaf parents had as good speech as deaf children of hearing parents, were better in reading and writing, and 38% of them went to college versus 9% of

---

23. Brill, presentation.

24. Stuckless and Birch, "Early Manual Communication," 452–462; G. W. Montgomery, "Relationship of Oral Skills to Manual Communication in Profoundly Deaf Students," *American Annals of the Deaf* no. 3 (1966): 557–565; Kay Meadows, "The Effect of Early Manual Communication and Family Climate" (doctoral dissertation, University of California, Berkeley, 1967); E. A. Stevenson, *A Study of the Educational Achievement of Deaf Children of Deaf Parents* (Berkeley: California School for the Deaf, 1964); S. P. Quigley and D. Frisina, *Institutionalization and Psychoeducational Development of Deaf Children*, Council of Exceptional Children. Research monograph series A, no. 3 (1961).

the other group.[24] At the California School for the Deaf in Riverside the average I.Q. of deaf children of deaf parents was 113. Of deaf children of hearing parents it was 104. This is statistically significant.[25]

Deaf children of deaf parents have had an effective communicating environment. Some schools for the deaf have decided to duplicate this type of environment to a certain extent during the vital preschool years. The California School for the Deaf in Riverside is one example. In only a few months' time, after using manual communication as well as speech and lipreading, some three-year-olds have developed as many as 300 usable concepts manually, while the typical number for a child using exclusively oral means is likely to be about 20 in the same period of time. The mothers come to school one day per week and use the total communication approach with their children at home. The children are happier and more relaxed and do not have that "blank" look. The mothers are highly enthusiastic because they and their children are really communicating.

I am hopeful that some day research will prove beyond the shadow of a doubt that the best way to educate deaf children is by the total communication approach. I like to visualize parents shifting from signs to fingerspelling to speech and lipreading or in combination according to the need, making sure that while they are communicating with other members of the family their deaf children know what is going on. I like to visualize parents interpreting a television program fully, telling a joke or discussing religion and setting aside part of the day for speech and lipreading practice. I like to visualize deaf children in the classroom unrestricted in the medium in which they want to communicate. Forcing them to speak and lipread has often had an opposite effect, while with expanding awareness and knowledge they will be sufficiently motivated and receptive to take the initiative in learning such skills. Learning will be painless and fun. Learning will be the thing and with learning they will be better prepared to really "live in a hearing world."

---

25. R. Brill, "The Superior I.Q.'s of Deaf Children of Deaf Parents," *The California Palms* (December 1969).

IPO Resolution

Larry writes a critique of the Alexander Graham Bell Association (AGB) here. Today, the divide between the AGB and components of the deaf community remain as wide as ever.

The board of the International Parents Organization (IPO), a section of the Alexander Graham Bell Association (AGB), sent out a memo to all IPO Parents Groups. The memo included a resolution for a public relations program to promote an oral education for the deaf that was passed by the IPO board, a page of suggested presentation for public information contribution and a statement of IPO board committee on a firmer stand on oralism. Some parts of the memo are quoted here in order to give readers an idea of what was said and to follow the comments I have made. The resolution is as follows:

> Be it resolved that the members of IPO feel a definite need for a strong, consistent program in telling the story of oral education for deaf children. This must be done on a national basis by professional people in the field of public relations. We, of IPO, realize that a strong offense is the best defense for any challenge! Thus, the advantages and lifelong goals of lipreading, speech and the use of residual hearing for the deaf can best be upheld and promoted by positive press releases and articles published in proper national media on a sustaining basis and consistently throughout the year. We feel this can best be done and maintained by experienced people who have the mechanics, knowledge and established outlets for national releases.
>
> Therefore, be it resolved that IPO recommends that the Alexander Graham Bell Association for the Deaf hire the firm of Robert Carter Associates, Inc., 1914 Sunderland Place, N.W., Washington, D.C., to develop and execute this public relations program. The cost of these services would be $1000.00 per month or a total cost of $12,000 per year.
>
> Be it further resolved that if and when the Alexander Graham Bell Association for the Deaf obtains $6000.00 towards this project that IPO will obtain matching funds (or a like amount) for the total financing of this program.

The Deaf American (December 1970)

The Alexander Graham Bell Association advised IPO that the Western Electric Company, a subsidiary of American Telephone and Telegraph, has given a grant of $6000 to help implement the above resolution. It was stated in the memo to all IPO parent groups that the IPO is now charged with the responsibility of matching these funds.

Under "Suggested Presentation for Public Information Contribution" in the same memo, it was stated that there was a need to help us spearhead a national public information center which will give parents of deaf children the results of pertinent research into oral education. The information center would collect data which parents can use in evaluating the merits of an oral education as opposed to a manual education, so they can make a fair choice for their children. It (the public relations firm) would prepare articles, press releases, television commercials, etc., on a national basis to tell the story and to emphasize the importance of an oral education for all hearing impaired children . . . . Another important requirement for a deaf child is to start his educational process as young as possible. It is vital for both the parents and the child that this initial approach should use the method which will offer the greatest opportunity for developing the child's capabilities.

The memo to IPO parent groups under the hearing "Statement of IPO Board Committee on a Firmer Stand on Oralism—February 1, 1970" carried statements such as the following:

> Oralism is being attacked on many fronts . . . Articles are appearing which strongly advocate the use of non-oral methods in educational programs for deaf children. Results of research studies are being quoted in support of this view although the validity of the research is seriously in question . . . IPO affiliate is being challenged by a new parent group whose sole and express purpose is to pressure school authorities into including simultaneous teaching techniques and interpreters in classrooms . . . In California . . . parents desiring to have oral educational opportunities for their children are doing battle with local authorities who are implementing manual techniques . . . These situations are illustrative of a movement which appears to be **national in scope and deliberate in intent** . . . We would also ask the Alexander Graham Bell Association Board of Directors to seriously question the desirability of remaining affiliated with the Council of Organizations Serving the Deaf. This alliance appears to be dominated by those of the other persuasion who are using its offices for the furtherance of their own ends

in an unethical and, most probably, illegal manner. Continued affiliation could prove both embarrassing and damaging to our cause . . .

Reading the above resolution, one cannot help but wonder why it is necessary to hire a public relations firm. To play on the emotions of the uninformed? To beguile and mislead the public with Madison Avenue lingo? Is not truth its own best advertisement?

The articles appearing in newspapers and magazines with which the IPO board takes issue are, in reality, one of the few occasions when our side of the story has had a chance to be told. How often in the past have syndicated news articles and feature stories given the impression that little deaf children were learning to talk normally and to speechread with ease and facility? Press a hearing aid button and you can hear again! Need more be said on this?

But back to the resolution. Already there is a play on words, a catch phrase calculated to mislead. Take this statement "an oral education as opposed to a manual education . . ." There is no such thing as a manual education. No school or program for the deaf is without auditory training equipment and every child in every school is given an opportunity to develop speech and speechreading skills. Almost all teachers, in fact, are trained in oral techniques.

To what extent can things be twisted around? It is they, the oralists, who have never given parents a fair choice yet the above resolution states "so they can make a fair choice." How in the world can one, single method, one method for all children do what the resolution states, "offer the greatest opportunity for developing the child's capabilities"?

Research is finally catching up with what we deaf people knew, with what we have seen with our own people, with what we have seen with our own eyes, with what we have to experience with our own lives. Deaf children of deaf parents are everywhere for the members of the IPO board to examine if they question the validity of research studies showing them to have superior IQ's compared to deaf children of hearing parents, to be academically advanced and, wonder of wonders, to have equal speech and superior speech reading skills.

In any research undertaking priority should be given to how much can actually be speechread. If we deaf people did not know since they day we become deaf that speechreading for purposes of in-depth communication is an ineffective tool, both IPO and AGB people would have no problem. We would be leaping on their bandwagon and fattening the Alexander Graham Bell Association's membership rolls.

Why is the IPO being challenged by a new parent group? Why has this new parent group brought out their own newsletter "The Endeavor"? And why is the membership of this group numbering into the thousands? It is because parents have become more sophisticated, better informed and more aware that appearances can deceive. Associating more closely with deaf adults, they have come to appreciate our communication problems. They would consider it unthinkable to frustrate us further by precluding simultaneous teaching techniques and interpreters in classrooms. Some of these parents started manual communication early enough—during preschool years—which in effect placed them on par with the deaf parents of deaf children. Results were immediately beneficial. The children became more relaxed, less of a disciplinary problem and better able to learn. By comparing their deaf children with those other deaf children who were not allowed to use manual communication they began to see that the development of speech and speechreading skills were not held back.

What takes the cake is the IPO board's questioning of the desirability of staying affiliated with the Council of Organizations Serving the Deaf. It is tantamount to say "Stop the world, I want to get off." The COSD is made up of various associations and religious organizations of the deaf. In short, it is a mirror of the deaf people of all walks of life. The fact that all the affiliates except one (one guess) gave approval to what the COSD was doing in circulating realistic literature speaks for itself—it shows how the deaf themselves feel.

The IPO group, through their public relations firm, has a perfect right to go ahead and tell the oral side of the story but let us deaf people watch the way they go about it. In the past we would turn the other way when misleading statements were made. This time we should be wary and respond immediately whenever the occasion demands it. Let us watch out for and protest vigorously if an exceptional student is used as a model, if there is no distinction made between the prelingual and the postlingual deaf, onset of degree of hearing loss, type of school mentioned for comparison purposes, etc. For example, a school might have the finest auditory equipment and orally trained teachers but because it permits manual communication on the playground or when children are past their prime learning years it is labeled a manual school. Misleading phrases such as "this a hearing world and . . ." are ones that we especially should watch out for.

The point of the whole thing is this: Are we to allow the education, well-being, and happiness of deaf children to become the playthings of emotion? Can we solve the problem by resolutions? By hiring public consultant firms? Are the best interests of deaf children served when policy is set and action initiated by those whose experience with the deaf people is limited to the one deaf child they have? Would not parent boards and groups be in a better position to sift, weigh and judge if they went out and communicated with the consumer, that is, a cross section of the deaf people themselves? If they went out and studied in depth different types of preschool and school programs? If they went out to the clubs, organizations and associations of the deaf on a state and national level?

If the IPO board members took the time and trouble to go out and meet with the deaf (not only ODAS members) they will find us a warm and friendly people who are as much, if not more, concerned with the development of speech and speechreading skills. They may not agree with the approaches we feel should be taken to develop such skills and the order of priorities that should be set up for the best interests of the deaf child. They may not agree with us but it should be clear that our thinking and feelings have been honed on the battle front of experience. Are not those who are battle-scarred worth listening to?

I Was in Your House — To MDG

Although not there I was in your house
Since birth. How else could kindred souls
Mesh in epiphanies.

The same waves caressed us and we
Telegraphed the same messages.
Transients on this earth, the same desires
Engulfed us.

We had fire in our eyes and fought
The dragons that tried to bind our hands
And make our voices shiver in the night.
And then came the drive for homogeneity
When placement, the sacred banner,
Loomed over the clicking of the mind.

We grew old together and yet apart
Meeting in spots that dot the map
And there renewed the selfsame goals
That drove us from the start.

When the Big Sign comes to call
We shall go with broken heart
Not so much because we are afraid
But because the life we love we must
Leave behind and you and I can touch
No more.

Dinner Talk at
San Diego, California

I went to a baseball game. There were 41,198 persons in attendance. So what happens? I am seated near a man who loves to talk. Out of 41,196 persons who can hear this man decided to select what was probably the only deaf person in the whole ball park to talk to.

My timing is beautiful. I push an elevator button. The door opens. I politely wait for someone to step out. He is holding a can of paint and as he steps out, for some unaccountable reason, the can departs from his fingers and smashes onto the floor. The man did not notice that some of the paint got on the cuffs on my pants. Me, make a big issue of it? Waste of time. As usual, I forgot my pad and pencil. A few of the offender's teeth were missing. Speechreading was out.

Like I say, forget it. There are compensations. For instance, there was the time when I stood in line waiting to enter a Las Vegas nightclub. I was "hand talking" with wife and friends when the manager saw us. He gave us the best table in the house and told us to call on him for show reservations any time. Yes, any time! He had, you see, a deaf brother.

The sweet and sour comes to us deaf people as it comes to most anybody else. It is interesting the way we adjust ourselves to life's exigencies. I, for example, have refined mumbling to a fine art. Tired of being the victim of those who have the urge to talk, I would, in the opinion of my hearing son, mumble beautifully. When people who ask me questions hear me mumble they assume that I find their questions too difficult to answer so they stop talking altogether. This is exactly the effect I aim for when I know they are the type I could never speechread even in such life and death situations as when they are trying to tell me my fly is open.

Tonight I would like to talk with you about my feelings not only as a deaf person but as a teacher of deaf students. I work with precious human beings and I hope you will bear with me if I become too serious.

The Deaf American (February 1972)

We seem to be living in an anonymous age. The individual face and personality is lost in a sea of rioting people. I remember reading a newspaper account of a person who said that the death of 6,000,000 Jews was too staggering to grasp and understand. However, when the death of one Jewish baby boy was described—how he was taken from his mother's arms, thrown up in the air and shot—the whole horrifying, bloody senselessness of it all hit home.

Let us talk about the education of one deaf person—deaf Joe. Husky and nice looking, not only did he have athletic skills but also a sharp mind. You probably know a person who could take a motor or a television set apart and put it all back together again. This person could make sense out of a mass of blueprints and build a house from scratch. And, if something was off, he could think of ingenious ways to cut, trim or reshape until everything dovetailed beautifully. When I say deaf Joe's mind was like this I do not mean in a mechanical sense but in the ability to think and reason and to see relationships in spite of all the monkey wrenches thrown his way as he tried to climb up the educational ladder.

Raw brainpower was there with deaf Joe. It was there but he failed the college entrance examinations. There was one barrier he could not overcome and that was language. Of course, this is nothing new. If the deaf have one thing in common, it is language shortcomings.

If deaf Joe could hear, what would he be? A doctor? A lawyer? Instead, will he be just another statistic among the deaf who are underemployed? If so, why? Who is to blame?

Let us go back to early childhood. Deaf Joe remembers how he cried when his mother put him to bed, turned off the lights and left the room. He cried because he was afraid of the dark and did not want the lights turned off. He did not yet have the words and the speech ability to say "Leave the lights on." And his mother, hearing him cry, must have said to herself "Of course, he doesn't want to go to sleep. He is only 2½ years old and needs the sleep. Let him cry."

Deaf Joe could not hear familiar footsteps which would let him know his beloved ones were around. For him no gentle voices to soothe his fears, no reassuring words such as "Do not be afraid, mommy will always be near." If lullabies were sung or a Red Riding Hood story told to him all he would see was the opening and closing of a mouth. He was too young to concentrate on a small mouth for more than a few seconds. If he were lucky, a familiar face or two would come into the periphery of his vision and break the intensity of the silence surrounding him as he lay in his bed. At his age, the world is a bewildering place—there is so much that is new, so much that is unknown. In his frustration, deaf Joe would often cry himself to sleep.

When he was ill or when something was bothering him, deaf Joe did not know how to tell that to his mother, not in specific terms. When he wanted ice cream or a glass of water he would take his mother's hand and lead her to where he could point to the thing desired. But when he was away from home, riding in a car for example, there was nothing to point at. Feelings became bottled up. Planted were the seeds of emotional problems. Frustration followed upon frustration and then deaf Joe's world exploded. In rage and fury he picked up a lamp and threw it, kicked or bit whatever was in his way, or he withdrew into himself and found refuge in the fantasies of his mind. He would get even with his parents and refuse to be toilet trained. Or he would refuse to pay attention to his teacher at school and as a grown boy he would continue to act babyish. In a place of employment, he would be given instructions by his foreman, instructions that he could not understand. He was older now and more in control of his emotions but he would look at the sea of hearing persons around him and silently mutter to himself: "Burn, hearie, burn!"

Deaf Joe would like to forget the years of emotional starvation and think of his education and whatever mental stimulation he had. He remembered going to the zoo as a child. He had no way of naming and classifying the animals because when his mother opened her mouth to speak he could catch only a word or two here and there. What he saw was mostly tongue, teeth and air. With little input he could not dress his thoughts in words. For example, one animal at the zoo was swallowing food and regurgitating it and Joe was curious and wanted to ask his mother to please explain what it was doing but no words came. If his mother had said "crocodile" he would never have distinguished the word on the lips.

Looking back, deaf Joe now knows that if his mother had used her hands and made the sign for "crocodile," two hands coming together like snapping jaws, the association between the hand symbol and the reptile would have been unmistakable. He would be getting input richer and superior than the spoken word which, in contrast to the animated movement of the hands, seems dull and lifeless. With hearing gone, Joe's eyes took up extra burdens especially in observing the expressions on the faces of people and the actions they make. Snapping hands were highly visible, something to turn around in his mind, a vibrant symbol upon which to hang the memory of what he had seen at the zoo. At home he could have made attempts to recall and discuss some of the animals with his mother who could have pointed out their pictures in a book. Talking with the hands is not society's way but the input and output, the stirring of the memory and the mental stimulation could lead to the desire to learn the printed word, society's language.

Deaf Joe would have liked to speak the word "crocodile" but at two or three years of age it was extremely difficult to say. Attempts could have been made to teach him but it is not as easy to say as a "top" or a "shoe" and the outcome, more likely than not, would have ended in exhaustion and frustration. The pleasure and joy of communicating would have gone and deaf Joe's brain would have signaled that it was better to keep his mouth shut.

When deaf Joe was older, perhaps six or seven years of age, he might finally have learned how to speak the word "crocodile." But at two or three years of age, an age of wonder and exploration, many thoughts buzzed through his mind and cried for immediate expression. Because his method of communication was restricted, by those who were older and stronger and who could hear, to speech and speechreading he felt like a person trapped in a small room who keeps pounding on a door and yelling "Let me out! Let me out!"

Deaf Joe went to school. He thought things would be different now. Everybody was trained and they were supposed to know a lot about deafness and deaf people. He was fitted with a hearing aid because using his remaining hearing was important. Like those at home and the people in the world outside, the teacher did not use her hands at all when talking. He was supposed to understand teacher's talk by speechreading together with the use of his hearing aid. His teacher's teeth and lips were formed in such a way that only a few spoken words came into view and were recognized. Sound came to him through his hearing aid but it was like screams and whistling. When he turned his hearing aid on higher he began to feel and not hear sounds. He could not make out many words nor hear connected speech. Everyone in the classroom was different—one could hear more, another less; one could speechread well, another not at all.

In the classroom the teacher took charge. Deaf Joe was expected to sit quietly in a little chair. "Look at my lips," the teacher says. "Show me a ball." After many repetitions and imitations, deaf Joe was able to copy what the teacher wanted him to. He could not help but feel he was some kind of animal trained to jump over a hoop.

Deaf Joe's language thus never had a chance to develop. He could not blame the members of his family. No one supplied them with information and they never had a chance to be in a position to make wise decisions. He could not be hard on his teachers. That was the way they were trained.

Edwin Markham's poem "The Man with the Hoe"[26] seems appropriate here. I hope you will forgive me for changing slightly the first two lines:

> Bowed by the weight of centuries he holds
> His hearing aid and gazes on the ground,
> The emptiness of ages in his face . . .
> Stolid and stunned a brother to the ox . . .
> Whose breath blew out the light within this brain . . .
> O masters, lords and rulers in all lands,
> Is this the handiwork you give to God . . .
> How will you ever straighten up this shape;
> Touch it again with immortality . . .
> O masters, lords and rulers in all lands,
> How will the future reckon with this Man?
> How answer his brute question in that hour
> When whirlwinds of rebellion shake all shores?
> How will it be with kingdoms and with kings—
> With those who shaped him to the thing he is—
> When this dumb Terror shall rise to judge the world
> After the silence of the centuries?

The breath that blew out the light within deaf Joe's brain came from many places. It came from some administrators, educators, parents, heads

---

26. Edwin Markham, "The Man with the Hoe," *San Francisco Examiner*, January 15, 1899. The author was inspired to write the poem after seeing the painting *L' homme a la houe* by the French artist Jean-Francois Millet.

of teacher training programs. I am not advocating that we rise up against the masters, lords, and rulers in our field but that we become more involved and make them more accountable for what they do.

It seems strange to me that some people in our field are constantly saying that talking with the hands is the easy way out and therefore should not be allowed—as if being deaf is not difficult enough. Using their voices is the easy way for these people. They, therefore, should not talk unless stones are put in their mouths. In our field, adults such as these are the problem and not the deaf children. Easy ways should be found for children to learn. Learning should be pleasurable and exciting. Also, communication with family members and others should be carried on with a minimum of strain and a maximum of joy. When our forefathers wrote that the pursuit of happiness is one of the inalienable rights of man, they did not intend to exclude the deaf.

If we intend to help future deaf Joes avoid emotional traumas, communication starvation and educational mediocrity we will have to establish practical objections and plans of action. I will touch on just two areas.

Parents play the most important role in their deaf child's life. Situations that are practical and meaningful occur in the home. In fact, nowhere else is there a more effective learning environment yet when parents try to get to first base with their child they are given a toothpick instead of a baseball bat. Who is going to equip them with enough knowledge and information so that they can make good decisions and wise choices?

Teacher training programs play a vital role in shaping and molding the destinies of us deaf people. Too many of them have been speech-speechreading-auditory-oriented. It is not the same thing to have this as part of the program and to be biased in this respect. Teacher training programs were established to train teachers and not to dictate policy. Schools and programs are the ones who decide policy yet on one side we have schools which use total communication and on the other side teacher training programs that exclude anything that has to do with manual communication.

You adult deaf citizens of San Diego have wonderful hearing friends here such as those associated with the Paul De La Cruz Memorial Foundation, those working at the Salk Institute and some educators in this city. Our deaf Joes cannot help but benefit with all of you working together. Believe me, deaf Joes throughout our country are waiting for us to cast off "the silence of the centuries."

Talks Before Parent Groups

I cannot help but be amazed and pleased that more and more of us deaf adults are asked to speak before parent groups. Only a few years ago we had difficulty being given a chance to be "heard" while those who were "paper smart" were usually asked to speak. We still are seldom, if at all, invited to speak before parent groups that have strong oral leanings. This is unfortunate because such groups need to be more broadly informed, to hear the other side of the story discussed and ventilated and to be aware that many of us deaf adults can bring to them the smell of reality.

I have noticed in many speaking engagements that deaf adults are becoming more involved. They attend to publicity, prepare refreshments, do the necessary leg work, appear and mingle with parents at meetings. This is a commendable and vital part in our march forward to better education for our deaf people.

Because my talks are too long to appear in one column I have divided them into two parts. The second part, which deals with my deaf daughter, will appear in next month's column. The following talk is a composite or adaptation of talks given at Las Vegas, Nevada; at Tucson, Arizona; and at Redlands and San Diego, California:

The moon se levait au-dessus du Rhone. A man qui descendait at this moment par un chemin etroit des Vosges, had just perceived it a travers les feuilles.

If you did not know French, did you strain to understand what was being said? Did you hear the comforting English words only to be irritated by the French ones? Did discomfort or uncertainty bother you? If your answer is yes, then you have some idea of what it means when we deaf people try to read the lips. When you heard the word "descendait" perhaps you thought of the English word "descend" while at the same time cocking your ears for the other French words that followed. If we tried to do the same thing, other words would have come by rat-a-tat-tat and our eyes would have missed them all.

The Deaf American (June 1972)

If you, dear parents, could develop a sense of the difficulties involved in speech reading you will be taking a giant step in understanding one of the biggest problems we have in our role of a deaf person. We wish, oh how we wish, it was simple to speechread. Because, for the majority of us, there are too many insurmountable barriers when it comes to speechreading we are forced to use, invent or sneak in other visual clues. The alternative would be to choke in our own silence, to suffer mental stagnation or to become paranoid.

Groups of parents, educators, in fact, the whole and allied fields in the education of the deaf, are split because we deaf people ourselves sought and fought for alternative visual clues, the greatest and most common of which is the language of signs.

A mother who shouts "I want my deaf child to go with hearing people and be like hearing people" should carefully weigh her words against what I have said and against the background reality of the world-at-large. So should many educators who use catch phrases such as "This is a hearing world and the deaf must live in a hearing world."

Of course, we know that the world is full of hearing people and that they do not talk with their hands. If we cannot speechread most of them, if we cannot turn on the television set and follow the dialogue, if we cannot attend the opera then what alternative do we have?

Should not every effort be made to see that deaf people are educated? Educated deaf people can enjoy poetry instead of hearing music. Educated deaf people can enjoy books and magazines instead of staring blankly at a television set. Educated deaf people can think and thus adapt, cope and live productively in a world of the hearing.

Is it not time that we deaf people are no longer looked upon as if we were disembodied beings with mouths and ears and protruding eyes floating around? Instead, should not primary consideration be given to our thoughts, our feelings, our emotions and, above all, to our happiness?

I wear three hats—as a deaf adult, as an educator for 22 years and as a parent of a three-year-old deaf girl. I will be talking with you wearing a combination of the three hats but mostly as a parent.

From the vantage point of one parent to another, how can I help you? I find that too many parents are not given enough information or they are given misleading information.

In no other field is it so easy to be deceived as in the education of the deaf. In few other fields are there so many variables that defy identification unless one is an expert.

Parents should be aware of how things really are and not what they appear to be. When we say this child is hard of hearing, what do we mean? In terms of hearing sounds or in terms of hearing and understanding connected speech? The distinction is important because if the child hears only sounds the learning environment is not going to be effective if too much dependence is placed on oral-aural methods alone.

Parents should be aware that there is a difference between using oral-aural methods part of the time and using them to the exclusion of all other methods. I know of one school for the deaf where a teacher uses the same auditory training methods employed at a top oral school for the deaf. The five-year-old children in her class go through auditory training for a brief period of time twice a day. The teacher covers her mouth and the profoundly deaf children with the help of auditory trainers try to detect the syllables and the words. A great deal of success has been achieved. The difference here is that the teacher uses other methods of communication, including manual communication, the rest of the time.

My question is: What research study is there that shows one must use oral-aural methods at all times in order to achieve success? Many schools and programs for the deaf have not adopted total communication and implemented under its umbrella the best of what top oral schools have to offer.

You will hear the argument that it takes a great number of years of concentrated effort and persistent practice sessions with oral-aural methods before success can be achieved. What does the deaf child do in the meantime, in the here and now, when he cannot understand connected speech? Are optimum learning conditions during critical years to be suspended until the child is able to cope by purely spoken, verbal, auditory means?

Parents should realize that if some children do well in one-to-one communication situations it does not automatically follow that it still will be true in group sessions such as in the classroom. Also, the contents of communication should also be taken into account. When contents or subject matter is kept on a simple level parents can be fooled into thinking that their child is "oral." The true test comes when topics are on a more complex level and when a lot of thinking and reciprocal discussions are involved.

Parents are told that every deaf child has some residual hearing which should be utilized. Fine, but again—to what extent? The argument goes that the utilization of residual hearing together with speechreading is all that is needed for effective communication functioning. Here, again, parents can be misled. If one has impaired hearing then sounds become muffled or distorted. To have residual hearing does not mean to hear in the speech frequency range. Also, one child may develop a knack for reading the lips while another will stare uncomprehendingly while you yell "Fire! Fire!" with all the clarity your lips can muster.

Each child is different in his or her receptivity to learning. One child can catch on to some skill or concept before you can bat an eyelash while another needs several repetitions. One child may have emotional problems while another may have brain, neurological or other physical handicaps.

Yes, each hearing impaired child is as different as a fingerprint or a snowflake.

There is something deeply and seriously wrong when a school or program for the deaf follows a single method of communication. In such a school you are likely to see mechanical learning. Progress is based on imitation and repetition and there is a greater chance that the child will become a parroting rather than a communicating personality.

When we talk about total communication we are talking about a recent phenomenon in the sense that manual as well as oral-aural methods are using during the preschool years and by parents in the home. Perspective is needed when we compare different school programs. We have never had until recently schools and programs that encouraged the inclusion of manual communication during preschool or the early, vital learning years. Rare was a teacher training center that offered manual communication courses. I am happy to say that the trend is changing. Take one revealing example—the National Association of the Deaf has published a manual communication book of which 25,000 copies have been sold so far.

I hope to live to see the day come when a top oral school will begin to utilize manual communication methods as a supplementary part of their program. Drastic changes will have to be made when we realize that by the time most deaf people reach adulthood they have not mastered the shape, sound, and sense of primary language of America—oral English.[27] Only 12% of the deaf people achieve true linguistic competence and only 4% become proficient speech readers or speakers.[28]

English is like a foreign language to the deaf. Parents should read the uncorrected composition papers of high school students from any school or program for the deaf and be ready for a shock. If you ask a bright 17-year-old deaf student "What is your opinion of . . ." you might receive a blank look because he is likely not to know the meaning of the word "opinion." I know of a deaf person who was fired from his job for writing the following statement "I make fool you" and handing the note to the boss' wife. He really meant to say "I was teasing you."

What is needed are training centers for parents of deaf children that show how total communication can be used effectively in the home. Without family involvement a large part of the battle is lost because the deaf child is with the family earlier than he is at school and the home environment is far more meaningful.

In the meantime, I hope that you parents can find the time to associate with deaf adults. When you learn to communicate with them and get to know them as human beings you will be in a better position to help your own deaf child.

There have been many definitions made of total communication. I would like to include here a definition of total communication made by a deaf student.

The student said: "Total communication is love."

---

27. Schlesinger and Meadow, "Deafness and Mental Health," p. 175.
28. Ibid., p. 175.

On Reading Once Again

It is a well known and documented fact that the reading status of deaf students is mediocre, ranging from a third to a fifth grade level by the time most of them are nearly adults.

For obvious reasons, the ability to read should be the single most important area of concern in the education of the deaf yet not only do incorrect approaches seem to be taken but there appears to be a lack of concentrated all-out effort. Instead of experimentation, exploration or a crash program of some kind uniquely suitable for deaf students and well coordinated throughout the nation, we have approaches that are planned for hearing students who already have a language base or slight variations of such approaches.

Instead of experiential learning activities and a performance program, we have thick, beautifully written curriculum guides that are glanced over and left to languish on some shelf. Instead of having parents or dormitory counselors become interested, involved and given ways and means to be of help, the sole burden is often placed on teachers. That is, instructional objectives are not clearly defined and those involved made accountable for what has been done.

To be made accountable need not imply some kind of threat but, rather, an analysis of what has been done and a search for better approaches. For example, short, simple goals can be set for certain stages of reading and if they are not met an analysis taken to find out the reason. Is it because the content was too difficult? Is it because the children were not first given the necessary experiences so that the reading material would be within their frame of reference? That is, if they are going to read about the zoo, go to the zoo first. Is it because teachers made unclear presentations, did not communicate effectively or did not prepare properly? Is it because there were no follow-ups? Is it because children were moved on to the next stage without having mastered the previous one?

The Deaf American (July–August 1973)

It is possible, indeed, to make exhaustive analysis, take constructive remedial action, participate in discussions without making teachers lose their sense of security.

I am happy to state that there is a school for the deaf which is taking some steps to improve its reading program. During the summer of 1972 some of the principals and reading teachers of the California School for the Deaf, Riverside, met daily for five weeks to try a drastic improvement in the school's reading program.

We too often fall into the trap of inbreeding: learn from each other, talk to each other, invite speakers from our field and so on, forgetting that deaf children are children first and deaf second. The Riverside school invited a reading specialist, Dr. Van Metre of the University of Arizona, who is outside the education of the deaf, for the first two days of the workshop. She was the badly needed catalyst that got the workshop participants off to a good start. Dormitory counselors were invited to participate and ways explored on where they can be of practical help.

With Dr. Van Metre the workshop participants reached the conclusion that one language form is primary. With hearing children that is speech; with deaf children it is the sign language. All other forms of language related to the primary form are secondary forms. Reading and language are different processes and reading is a secondary process to primary language.

Dr. Van Metre's theme song was that of the new concept in teaching language: We learn by doing and by using it—not by learning *about language*. This is achieved through divergent activities (the type of activities that encourage a child to think and feel for himself) and through convergent activities (the type of reading activities that help improve knowledge and skills and which often call for a "yes" or "no" response).

The paramount concern of the workshop at the Riverside school was to prepare instructional objectives and produce a guide that is performance-oriented, something teachers can follow and carry out in their classrooms. Accountability, for both teacher and student, is part and parcel of the guide. The goals of the program will be further pursued in the form of in-service training during the school year.

It would be naïve to presume that there is a magic formula which can open the doors to reading success. Auditory deprivation brings with it a tremendous gap in normal learning development. It is a combination of approaches that can help, partially, to bridge the gap.

The parent approach is the most important because the child is in the home during his critical learning years. The parent is in a position to supply the experiences of having a cat or a dog, of going on a trip, of visiting relatives and hundred other happenings that can expand the child's world. The parent is in a position to communicate with the child all that is happening. Later on the child will be able to relate to what he reads, the input he has received, and all his experiences.

Parents are in a position to help, especially where reading readiness is involved, if only schools will design a practical program that tells them how. Parents can help their deaf offspring become aware of the printed word, trace letters in sand, cut and paste words and pictures. One parent of a five-year-old deaf girl, who has outstanding language ability, told me she would pick up an object such as a box, fingerspell it and ask her deaf girl to make the sign for it. Then the roles would be reversed with the child fingerspelling and the parent signing. Of course, speech and speechreading were also utilized. This same parent would play language games with her child. She would begin with the single word "box" then expand it to "the box," "the red box," "the big red box" and so on.

It is a sad fact that so few parents tell stories to their deaf offspring. High school members of the Riverside school's Junior National Association of the Deaf chapter have taken the role of surrogate-parents. They have been going to the dormitories of the younger students in order to tell bedtime stories. Those of us who are familiar with the short attention span of young deaf children would be amazed at the interest and concentration of these children when told stories they have never been told by their parents. Their enraptured faces were a sight to behold as stories from the moving hands of those deaf like themselves came across to them.

The aim has been to stir little deaf children, arouse their interest and curiosity, leave the storybooks that have been read to them in the dormitories for a while in the hope that the children themselves will make the effort to turn the pages of a book and go on from there.

There are schemes and ideas and programs that are running rampant in schools across the country. Each in itself can achieve, at best, partial success. What is needed is some kind of national clearinghouse or central agency that can receive a continuous stream of suggestions, ideas, projects. Such an agency can sift and try out promising concepts and radiate their findings to schools and programs for the deaf throughout the country.

With a preponderance of prelingual deaf children now in schools such a concerted effort is called for. This is not really asking too much when we want to bring deaf children "into the company of man."

A Total Communication Family

Newman's definition of Total Communication here is different than most people perceive. Instead of using speech and sign at the time, he advocates for using the communication modality that works best with the child. Here, he illustrates a family that cares and loves their deaf child and uses it as a standard.

Many of us, by now, are familiar with the comparative studies made of deaf children of deaf parents and deaf children of hearing parents. Such studies showed deaf children of deaf parents to be ahead in some aspects of academic achievement and in speechreading skills. The variable was the utilization of manual communication by deaf parents and none for all practical purposes, whatsoever by hearing parents. Now, however, we are becoming more acquainted with stories of hearing parents of deaf children who are utilizing total communication during the early critical learning years. There may have been isolated cases in the past but, make no mistake about it, the extent to which hearing parents are also signing to young deaf children is a recent phenomenon.

A case in point is the family of John and Fleana Snapp. Rachel, now five years old and the youngest of their four girls, is deaf, a rubella child with an 80–85 db loss in each ear. How they started on total communication is an interesting story. The family was in Washington, D.C., attending Gallaudet College's preschool program. John, the father, is a lieutenant colonel in the army and a sharp-eyed observer. He asked his wife to observe the intensity and quality of communication going on between a mother and her daughter at the preschool clinic. The mother turned out to be the late Judith Williams, a deaf woman, utilizing the simultaneous method in communicating with her deaf daughter, Tiffany.

It did not take the Snapps long to recognize that the variable was manual communication. As unobtrusively as they could, they asked Rachel's teacher, Connie Yanconne, to help them communicate as the deaf parents did. She obliged. John, however, soon received orders to be

The Deaf American (April 1973)

on duty on the West Coast. Immediately, they pressed for the start of a class for 18-month- to three-year-old deaf children on the Monterey Peninsula in California. Bureaucratic machinery is well-oiled. Her request was passed from one bureaucrat to another—"Classes for the very young deaf, what do they need it for?" "Wait until they are three years old," "Put them with other handicapped children," "Integrate them with hearing children," "We do not have enough deaf children—ok, if you can find me not less than six deaf children we'll start a class for the 18-month–three-year-old deaf children." They thought Mr. Snapp would never find that many deaf children on the Monterey Peninsula. They did not reckon with Fleana, a greatly determined woman.

Like a collector with a net in pursuit of butterflies, Fleana Snapp roamed the Monterey Peninsula. Every time she caught sight of a child with a hearing aid her heart pounded and she became engulfed in animated conversation with the parent. To the consternation of the bureaucrat who challenged her, Fleana presented him with the names and addresses of six deaf children. A class was started and a year later Connie Yanconne came to California. Connie and her husband are northern Californians and the lure of greener pastures was irresistible. When Fleana asked her to accept a teaching job in Monterey, a call to the County Office of Education paved the way for her new job.

Connie Yanconne is a marvelous, gifted teacher who has tried the oral method, cued speech and settled on total communication as the most suitable method to meet the individual needs of deaf children. Young but insightful beyond her years, she emphasized family involvement, a sensitivity for the communication needs of young deaf children, and she made many suggestions for learning activities in the home.

In the meantime, the Snapp family, the whole bunch of them, became immersed in learning total communication. They learned the new form with its verb endings, distinguishing tense forms, signs for "he, she, they, him," signs for words where there was none before. Rachel was encouraged to use her speech at all times and everyone used his speech when signing to her. Of course, auditory input was not overlooked and Rachel constantly wore her hearing aid. They remembered the admonitions of Connie Yanconne to fingerspell if they did not know the sign for a word.

It is one thing to use total communication when the deaf child is involved and another thing to use it with other hearing members of the family in the presence of the deaf child—in other words, the creation of a communicating environment so that the deaf child will see what otherwise she would hear of the incidental communication going on.

Mrs. Snapp was busily talking to one of her girls when she felt Rachel tugging at her. She ignored Rachel and went on talking to her hearing daughter. She felt a more forceful tug and was about to turn around in order to tell Rachel to wait when she saw tears in her deaf daughter's eyes. Rachel was finally able to say "Mommy, you are not signing."

From that day on, everyone used signs as well as speech when talking to each other. Everything spoken was also signed, even swear words. At the dinner table, the family played sentence games. One member would say "box." Another member would say "The box." A third member would say "The box is." A fourth member would say "The box is big." At another time Fleana would fingerspell a word and then ask Rachel to sign it. Roles would be reversed—Rachel would fingerspell a word and her mother would give the sign for it.

Phrases, expressions, idioms, sayings, spoken descriptions of everyday common occurrences were communicated to Rachel.

This was the background scene when I first entered the home of the Snapps and met five-year-old Rachel. Although I had been warned about Rachel, for instance, when she was three years old Roy Holcomb told me she had no equal for language sophistication, I still was not prepared for what I witnessed.

Rachel is a cute, beautiful, personable human being. Her mother spelled my full name, my wife's full name and the names of three other persons I had brought along with me. Her mother spelled the names only once and Rachel could spell them back instantly. Flames were shooting up in the fireplace of the living room. My eyes almost popped out when Rachel said "The fire is blazing." She used the new sign[29] for "the," the Ameslan sign for "fire," the new sign for "is" and because there was no sign the family knew for "blazing" she fingerspelled this word and all the while she was vocalizing.

Rachel dazzled us with sentence after sentence that any normal hearing child would use. We brought along our three-year-old deaf daughter,

---

29. Newman is referring to the Signed Exact English version of these signs. For instance, "the" is signed with the manual sign for "T".

Carol, and they both hit it off at once. They played together all night. The hunger for companionship one deaf person has for another deaf person was no less true here than two hearing children attracted to each other by some common bond. I remember when I was a boy and was given a basketball for my birthday, I went to the school yard. There were hearing children everywhere but I soon found it was my basketball they wanted and not me.

When it was time to leave I invited Rachel to come and stay with us. This was a mistake. She wanted to come with us right then and there and Carol joined in the insistent chorus.

Fleana Snapp tried to reason with Rachel. "Not tonight. We will visit them some other time."

"WHY?" Rachel snapped. Mrs. Snapp replied "Santa Claus is coming and he'll be confused on where to leave the presents."

"He will not be confused," Rachel quickly responded, using the new sign for the past tense of "confuse." Then she said and this put us all in stitches "I am going to have a fit." She tapped her shoe on the floor as she said this. "Stop tapping at me," her mother said. Then Rachel did not sign at all. Instead, a torrent of words was voiced by her. She was pouting and shouting just like a hearing child. It was beautiful. The family spat was just like any other family spat.

"I want to go to Carol's house," Rachel kept insisting. "Now." Our Carol put her nose in. "With me, my house now." Suddenly, they both ran upstairs. I followed them up, huffing and puffing. I carried down a kicking, punching Carol. Everybody downstairs tried hard not to laugh.

I felt light and gay. My heart was lifted up. For over 20 years I deeply felt that if only a family were totally involved in the communication process that included manual communication, the deaf child will have a chance to read and write, to sing and drink deep of the springwaters of life. For generations, almost all young deaf children went through oral methods only during their critical learning years. Now there are families like the Snapps in Montana, in Monterey, in Minnesota, in Chicago, in Maryland, in Pennsylvania, almost everywhere. Perhaps the effects will snowball. At long last, there is some hope for the educational well-being of our deaf children.

I asked the Snapps why not expose your child, let the world see the miracle they have achieved, let the world know that manual communication and speech can co-exist, that the one can facilitate the acquisition of the other.

The Snapps are modest and cautious people. "We do not want to become a traveling carnival." Mr. Snapp has many irons in the fire. He feels that the current parent organizations in California are not achieving their goals. He feels that a new, statewide parent organization firmly committed to the total communication philosophy is necessary to accomplish the objective of a total education for deaf children. He wants to enter the Leadership Training Program at California State University, Northridge and in the years ahead find a position where he can reach the most people in the least amount of time.

As for myself, I want to jump on every rooftop and announce what has come to pass. I want to spread the glad tidings.

President's Remarks

We try to keep abreast of what goes on in the field of deafness. There are three areas that are having a national impact:

1. An intensified approach to auditory training;
2. Mainstreaming or the placement of hearing impaired children in classes with hearing children; and
3. The changeover to Total Communication on an increasing scale in many schools and programs for the deaf.

[. . .] Exciting developments are occurring in the field of audiology. Our technical society is making possible advances in amplification equipment. Behind the ear hearing aids are now as powerful as body aids once were and it is possible to custom fit hearing aids for each child. Curriculum guides geared to help children develop listening skills as early as possible are now available. At the present time we have equipment that stimulates what your hearing impaired child hears, that tells us how his or her hearing aid functions, that diagrams middle ear functioning to determine whether or not medical attention is needed, etc. Scientists, engineers, physicists and otologists are continuing to experiment with implanted aids so that even those with nerve deafness, hopefully, will be able to hear.

We must guard ourselves against the contention that if started early enough and if properly fitted, hearing aids will bring our children close to or up to the level of hearing children. Hearing sound is not the same as understanding connected speech. Hearing loss varies in so many ways and there are so many factors involved that we cannot predict to what extent each child will benefit. What a child can hear in a one to one or small group situation or in an acoustically treated room is different when placed in the real world of rackets, discords, and garbled speech.

What I am trying to point out is that auditory training under the umbrella of Total Communication is an important and worthwhile

Speech, International Association of Parents of the Deaf Fourth Biennial Convention, Washington DC, August 8, 1975 endeavor. Unnecessary risks are taken in terms of emotional and psychological stability when auditory training is looked upon as having the goal of a sole method of communication or a thing apart.

Mainstreaming has been done in the past under the term "integration." Now, under new legislation and under the cry that *every* handicapped child has the right to be educated, we are going to see more of this concept.

To understand mainstreaming, one should view it from the context of the strong feeling that handicapped children should not be isolated from society. This has great merit. *But,* where deaf people are concerned, we must remember that the handicap is not merely physical. It is a language and communication handicap. Why would deaf children be better able to develop language and communication skills by being placed in the mainstream rather than in a class of 6 or 8 children with a trained teacher of the deaf? Is it realistic to expect that a deaf child, placed in a class of 30 to 40 hearing children, will be able to speechread what is going on and be able, with all the noise, to utilize his hearing aid effectively? With a few deaf students in a large public school are there going to be enough people who care, who are knowledgeable about the needs and problems of the deaf? Are there going to be sufficient funds so that children will have speech therapy, audiological assessment, interpreting and other support services? Will our deaf children be able to wade through a series of frustrations, academically and socially, and still be able to develop a healthy sense of self? Or will they try to pass themselves off as a black man trying to be a white man in a white society?

This is *not* to imply that every deaf child placed in the mainstream will drown. With careful planning and appropriate support personnel, I do not question the fact that some hearing impaired children can make a go of it in classes for the hearing.

We must rid ourselves of the notion that once Total Communication is utilized, all of our ills will vanish. There are so many factors involved: intelligence, additional handicaps, prior schooling, type of family involvement, and so on. Make no mistake about it, however, Total Communication is the best approach we have because for once it is flexible enough to accommodate the varying needs of our hearing impaired children instead of having them accommodate us big adults. Total Communication has been attacked as a smokescreen for manualism or just another name for the simultaneous method. It is said that programs utilizing Total Communication neglect aural-oral skills. If this is true then it is not the fault of Total Communication per se, but the program that professes to be carrying it out.

We know of deaf children of deaf parents who attend schools where aural-oral methods are used exclusively. They usually stand out in such schools because they have had language input and an understanding of many concepts via sign language from their deaf parents. In addition, they have excellent speech and speechreading training from their schools. In other words, they have had the best of two worlds. This is what a model Total Communication school would be trying to implement.

With a prelingual deaf population beset with additional handicaps and with a wide spectrum of individual differences, sign language has proved itself to be a powerful learning tool. It has lessened frustrations, promoted emotional stability, acted in many different ways as a bridge to the hearing world.

There is a lovable lady, a world-renowned linguist at the Salk Institute in San Diego, California, Dr. Ursula Bellugi, who has studied American Sign Language for a number of years. Her aim was to understand the nature of human language. Not only has she found that ASL is a rich, full language with the basic characteristics of any human language, but that it also has very special, unique and individual properties because of its development as a visual rather than an auditory language. She emphasizes that deaf people should have a "sense of pride in the language they have developed . . . that deaf people have demonstrated their intelligence, uniqueness, and abilities in the development of a language of their own." She goes on to state that hearing people have discovered "the wonder and beauty and power of the language of the deaf . . ." She feels that it is important for deaf people, as well as for hearing people, to know that the special ability that makes man unique from all animals—the ability to develop language—has flourished in a very rich way in the deaf in their sign language, as it has in hearing people in the 5,000 or more spoken languages of the world.

Dr. Bellugi's words make me feel good. In the past we felt we stood alone and always had to defend what we were doing and in what we believed. Now we have parents such as you on our side. We can communicate with you on a scale unknown before. Your children need not be limited to "How are you? I am fine." They can ask you questions on why clouds, sun and moon move in space. They can come closer to you and be a real member of the family.

Finally, in all our talks, decisions, actions, do we ever pause and ask ourselves: what are we living for? What is life all about? And if our stay on earth is but like a brief candle, then what is our primary goal? The pursuit of happiness is one of the inalienable rights of man. Could we sum it up by stating that we will do everything we can to encourage our deaf children to reach for happiness and to be happy?

President's Corner:
A Deaf Child in a Hearing Family

No question about it, a deaf child faces formidable obstacles when every member of his family is hearing. In terms of dealing with the handicap of deafness, each member is more likely than not to be totally unprepared. Practically every action and reaction, the thinking processes, the emotional expressions have evolved from existing in a world of sound. Perspectives and perceptions have developed from the vantage point of sound.

In this type of family, the deaf child's raw emotions surface in order to satisfy basic needs. Unfortunately, these emotions usually find outlets in physically acting out or in tantrums. At this point in time, who can blame the deaf infant for trying to find a means to satisfy basic needs? Unheard are the soothing reassurances of the mother or the balm of familiar sounds which are distinctive to each family member.

The [wheelchair-bound] need crutches or a wheelchair, the blind Braille, persons with other disabilities need—if not prosthetic devices— doses of patience or strategic approaches to lessen the severity of their handicaps. It can be shouted from every roof or every mountaintop, but it tends to be neglected or glossed over—the deaf need effective and meaningful communication.

Sadly, which road the family travels—aural/oral, total communication, cued speech, verbotonal—depends on whom they sought out first or which professional caught their ears first. Shades of brain-washing.

It would be ideal if each family could have intensive and extensive orientation not only to the various methods of communication but to the nature of deafness itself and its by-product problems. It would be ideal if there were a central storehouse of information in each state, if families were given the opportunity to meet their "children grown"—deaf adults of various stripes and shades.

NAD Broadcaster (February 1988)

In the meantime, let us go back to the deaf child in his or her world of today—what additional barriers are set up if the family is Spanish speaking? Or Oriental? Or single parents burdened with the need to make ends meet? Or two working parents who come home tired from a long day at work? Or parents who have their hands full with other siblings?

At a Jr. NAD[30] workshop many years ago, deaf teenagers expressed their feelings about their families. One recalled that her parents were nice, took her on field trips, but did not explain anything. Another mentioned that there was little or no direct communication from her parents. Instead it went indirectly from brother to her, thus casting this sibling in the role of third parent. She cried out, "My parents explain everything to my hearing brother or sister but not to me." A shy, but personable youngster exclaimed, "My parents are getting a divorce, but they do not tell me why." And there was this teenager who revealed—during pre-captioning times—that she offered her mother ten dollars to interpret a television program.

When I was principal of a day school program more than 10 years ago, I could observe a class and immediately know which students had involved and communicating families simply by the way they were interacting with the teacher. With the current, enlightened attitude to various modes of communication there might be more interaction taking place with deaf children in hearing families than used to be the case two decades ago. I am sure, however, that there are far more deaf children in hearing families today who are not benefiting from the critical role of family interaction than those who are.

I am trying to point out that at the outset deaf children are several steps behind their hearing peers which, of course, most of us know. Most of us know that the language and reading gaps can be traced to the absence of meaningful communication during the critical growing up years. But do most families know of the critical role they play? Do they realize the onerous burden placed on schools and programs for the deaf which must try to make up for the void created by non-communicating families?

In terms of the larger picture, are officials on the state and federal level doing enough in the area of funding and the publicizing of the critical

---

30. The youth branch of the National Association of the Deaf.

need for each intervention? Do they realize that a generic approach to school placement decisions seriously impairs the efforts of deaf people who are trying to make up for the gaps in their early lives?

I am hoping that the Commission on the Education of the Deaf will place the education of families with deaf children on the top priority list which will result in a clearinghouse of information in each state and a nationwide effort to reach and help educate such families.

Part Four

ON A MIXED BAG —
COLUMNS AND
POETRY ON
(A) DEAF LIFE

Columns

Newman's poems are beautiful yet efficient, and they humanize the deaf experience by offering unique perspectives into his world. In this part, as well, we see his fresh perceptions of the Deaf President Now movement and the skirmishes he fought as president of the National Association of the Deaf. Here, Newman's humanism stands out in contrast to the dominant medical and pathological viewpoints of the day.

At Gallaudet, Mervin Garretson, Newman's contemporary, was a poet of some note. Later, in Riverside, Newman's counterpart Felix Kowalewski also wrote poetry. When asked why he wrote poetry, Newman explains, "Poetry is the music of a deaf man's soul. I have had it in me since I was small. Arts must have an audience and they must be put on display. The form of poetry allows me to express thoughts and show that being deaf doesn't prevent me from writing well. I was also determined to write poetry into adulthood so parents of deaf children would know that deaf people could write."

Through the poems here, we can learn more about Newman's reaction to the narrow approach of the times. He wrote "Ballet of the Hands" as a response to the oral method. In "Girl with a Whirligig," he offers a note of hope at the end.

Recreation and Entertainment: Yesterday — Today — Tomorrow

Some characteristics of people are so universally akin in that most of them seek recreation and entertainment after a steady diet of work. Due to communication factors the after-work outlets for the deaf are a little narrower yet more broad than a large segment of the hearing public would suspect.

"Can the deaf swim?" asked a university student preparing her thesis. Whereupon the secretary-treasurer of the National Association of the Deaf penned an answer that should be a classic: "In order to swim I suppose we must paddle with our ears."

The deaf have an urge to identify themselves with hearing counterparts in habits of recreation and entertainment whenever possible but there is seldom any deviation from the ordinary. What makes the situation different is that the deaf would rather use more of these habits among themselves than with the hearing public. The reasons are easily apparent: among their own kind communication problems disappear and similar handicaps open up a fount of mutual understanding.

It would be interesting to learn that the deaf of the older generation sought basically the same kinds of recreation in use today—hobbies, sports, civic meetings, social gatherings—with new kinds and greater variety added to each field making up the main differences.

The do-it-yourself boom enlarged the hobby area. Coming increasingly into vogue have been golf and bowling and other departures from major sports. The trends in the civic meetings have been leaning more and more towards the national and the international, and together with a more liberal outlook on tobacco and alcohol at the social gatherings that would have shocked deaf grandmother have appeared such modern day innovations as charades and scrabble.

The Silent Worker (October 1954)

So notable are the deaf for manual dexterity that they will be found building or renovating their own homes in leisure time, dissecting and then assembling their television sets and other electrical and mechanical devices, shaping model airplanes, trains, or cars, sometimes entering them in local or national contests. Their hobbies range from common place stamp-collecting to hazardous airplane flying and unusual button-collecting. There is even one deaf lady with interesting literature and materials on human hands.

A glance through back issues of *The Silent Worker* will point out the variety and skill of the deaf in their number one recreation—sports. Almost every kind culminates in one tournament after another and the deaf who have attained public prominence are avidly followed. The American Athletic Association of the Deaf (A.A.A.D.), which is patterned along lines similar to the American Athletic Union (A.A.U.) is the great patron of amateur sports in the world of the deaf but unlike the A.A.U. and its great Olympic teams it could not send teams to the Olympics of the deaf held in Belgium last summer due to insufficient funds.

Almost every state in America has a kind of association or society that safeguards the rights of the deaf and these organizations little by little are becoming affiliated with an organization on a national level, the National Association of the Deaf. In increasing numbers deaf individuals are joining this NAD, which is actually a non-profit organization founded for their benefit, and there is a growing awareness of the world Federation of the Deaf which recently held a convention in Rome, Italy, with representatives from several countries, including America. Not to be overlooked are two other societies, one the established National Fraternal Society for the deaf, an insurance body, by, of, and for the deaf with local branches in almost every large city and town in the United States and several branches in Canada, and the embryonic Order of Desoms, an offshoot of the Masons. The average deaf person finds a kind of recreation in the meetings of these societies as well as in the state and civic organizations because throughout them dual purposes run: business and pleasure.

Benefit affairs have lately followed the time-honored traditions marking social gatherings—benefits for the home for the aged, for a club-house, or for trips for the basketball team. Card-playing from poker to pinochle, is ever popular at parties, but the highbrow set have introduced chess and checker affairs and other games appealing to the intellect. Remaining the most popular social gathering of them all whether in small or large groups are picnics. Picnics have been going on since perhaps the first sandwich was invented due no doubt to the fact that every member of the family can participate. Picnics have become more gigantic being state-wide and held during national conventions and they have been marked by barbecue pits and field days with prizes given to almost every entrant.

The deaf are probably among the world's greatest travelers. Vacations find them touring the country in their own automobiles, attending distant conventions, or flying to foreign lands.

Sadly, one recreation that has either remained static or decreased in usage is reading owing to the encroachments of television or a marked increase in the age-old problem of the deaf, language deficiency. Always few in numbers the deaf in prose and poetry writing have walked over a plateau down the years.

The movies and television are vying with each other for the number one spot in a deaf person's entertainment repertory.[1] The era of silent films offered little or no communication problems for the deaf but today they will be found at theatres displaying foreign films with English subtitles. Possessing gregarious tendencies, the urge often comes upon the deaf to go out and be with the crowd and thus they will be found in a movie theatre patiently watching an American film that makes no sense and laughing as the case may be in rhythm with the others to escape being singled out as something of an old grouch. The advent of television was a boon for the deaf. At last, the radio had been turned into a magic mirror whereby at the touch of a finger a kaleidoscope of action, scenery, and especially sports came into view. The sponsors of the latter events have kindly flashed scores and the names of the participants in ticker-tape fashion that the deaf may become one with the hearing in the enjoyment of such programs.

Some forms of entertainment that have lasted down the years are literary or dramatic events. Each generation has had its own Edwin Booth and there have been characters whose fingers would leave impressions on the air, whose hands would magically flash with meaning, whose

---

1. This is at least twenty years before captioned television became widespread.

facial expressions were so captivating that the deaf would be moved and excited and transported to another world, something that only the greatest soprano could similarly accomplish in the world of the hearing. Story-telling, poetry-picturization or poetry by rote, pantomimes, skits, plays have been presented in such numbers that it can be said they are recreation for the participants and entertainment for the audience. In this field the deaf reached a peak of achievement when some players from Gallaudet College presented *Arsenic and Old Lace* on Broadway in the same theatre where it was having its daily run.

In the past for their recreation and entertainment the deaf went to the basements of a number of churches where often large social gatherings and important literary events were held. Such a practice continues today but is not so prevalent. Halls, auditoriums, and gymnasiums are often hired, but most of the activities occur in club houses which are owned by deaf groups. The one in Los Angeles is three stories high and has its own bar, auditorium, lunch counter, and card room while the one in Pittsburgh is a simple single room affair where the deaf congregate just to bask in each other's company. Many of the clubs support a basketball team and sometimes bowling and softball groups. Many clubs have their own hall of fame where plaques and trophies and pictures of past officers of the club are prominently displayed.

Certain causes of deafness, especially spinal meningitis and mastoiditis, seem guilty of retarding some aspects of motor functioning of the deaf. A rather familiar sight is the deaf person who has difficulty walking properly at night and the deaf baseball outfielder misjudging a fly. However, in most areas of recreation and entertainment the deaf are limited mainly in those functions that require the use of hearing and unfortunately, too, the use of language. In do-it-yourself activities the deaf on the average are limited by inability to comprehend the technical instructions given. By trial and error, by the help of others, by common sense, or by a knack of discerning the necessary directions out of a jungle of words the deaf do in many instances surmount the difficulties.

In the years to come there is a strong possibility that the American Athletic Association of the Deaf will become financially strong enough to organize teams for the world Olympics of the deaf. The National Association of the Deaf might at last realize a full-time working staff and its actions might become expanded to include movements on an international level in conjunction, perhaps, with the World Federation of the Deaf. Although the wide technological advances of this generation have little affected the entertainment and recreation habits of the deaf, at least, in proportion to hearing persons, the future will tell a different story. The appearance of a kind of television-telephone combination with its easier communication possibilities for the deaf is just a matter of time. And there is this wonderful thing called tape-recording. A tiny transistor might power a contraption, large or small, that will print spoken words. The advantages that this will present for the deaf are almost limitless. One could be placed near the television set steadily interpreting the goings on and another could be carried at all times and instead of reading the lips the deaf would look at the machine as closely as a broker following the fluctuations of the stock market on ticker-tape. The constant presence of functional language might make it possible for the communication and language problems of the deaf to lessen if not entirely disappear thus closing even further the gap between the world of silence and the world of sound.

Our Public Image

I was introduced to a deaf man who visited my classroom more than two years ago. This man was the type who did not know any manual communication, who did not understand why the deaf had reading and language problems and who, it seemed, had only hearing people for friends. From his letter to me, it appeared that he was either employed at or did research work at the Socio-Behavioral Research laboratory of Pacific State Hospital, Pomona, California. He was doing an anomalous person experiment, that is, the attitude of the nondisabled toward the handicapped.

Perhaps some of us have wondered what the public thinks of us. How do they really size us up? The following finds are not comprehensive or final but they are interesting, nevertheless.

Included in the study were the amputee, wheelchair, blind, harelip, stutterer, deaf, palsied, retarded, mentally ill, homosexual. Asked if they would have us, the deaf, as their friend a little over 53% of those questioned said that they would. For purposes of comparison, we ranked sixth below the amputee, wheelchair, blind, harelip, stutterer. If it is any consolation, we ranked above the palsied, retarded, mentally ill and homosexual in that order. Nearly 80% said they would have the amputee as a friend. Over 66% said they would work with us, a sixth ranking again, compared to over 90% for the amputee. Over 80% said they would not mind living in the same neighborhood with us and over 94% said they would speak to us. In both instances, we ranked sixth in the same aforementioned order.

Now comes this shocker (or is it, really?): Only a little over 10% said they would marry us.

Now, now my friends, do not feel too badly. In this instance, we ranked third, below the amputees (18%) and the blind (16%). Apparently, our improvement in the standing is a triumph of human instinct. It is an acknowledgement that our hearing may be impaired but not our

---

The Deaf American (March 1971)

biological drive. Still, the fact that only 10% would marry us is disturbing, to say the least. It would not stand well with the proponents of integrating the deaf with the hearing. Gee, only 10%. Preliminaries are important, after all. The whisperings and cooings and such. It would not do to turn on the lights in order to speechread. Oh well, we should take satisfaction in the fact that none would marry the retarded and only 1% would marry the palsied or the homosexual.

Now that our ego or self-image has been deflated—temporarily, I trust, because we are a hardy people with great recuperative powers—what conclusion can be drawn?

The oralists might cry out: See! If the deaf put heart and soul into learning to speak and speechread there would be no such problems.

The total communication people might counter with: The deaf have done so the last 100 years. The way the deaf speak, the difficulties they have in speech reading might be the very things that cause them to rank sixth.

As a minority group we usually have to face the ingrained misunderstandings, misapprehensions or plain prejudices of those who are not familiar with us. Outlandish as they seem these preconceived notions are actually believed: All Mexicans sleep all day, all Japanese are gardeners, all Chinese work in laundries. When a person takes the effort to communicate with and get to know a Mexican, a Japanese or a Chinese a sort of individuality and a unique personality emerges. The longer one associates with and gets to know a person of a different race or color the more the differences tend to fade into the background.

In the field of education of the deaf, sad to say, because of the narrow one-method oral stance taken by teacher training centers we find the same misunderstandings, misapprehensions or plain prejudices among educators. Teachers, some of whom later become administrators, have been led to believe that those who use manual communication are mentally retarded or cannot use speech and if they can, well, their speech would have been much better if they never used their hands.

At a summer session in mathematics at Gallaudet College sponsored by the National Science Foundation in 1965, there were in one class over 50 hearing and deaf teachers of mathematics from day and residential schools for the deaf throughout the country. Unbelievably, for some day school teachers it was the first contact with the adult deaf, the first time they saw interpreters and had a chance to see manual communication in action. They could not believe they were witnessing highly intelligent and articulate deaf individuals. With their own ears they were hearing speech that was superior to the speech of those they taught back home and who never were allowed to use manual communication. They could not believe the intelligent contributions of the deaf in class discussions, they way they kept the professors, the nation's top authors and teachers of mathematics such as Meserve, Berger, Wirtz, Knipp, on their toes.

Some of the day school teachers began to learn how to fingerspell and to pick up a few signs here and there. So impressed was one day school teacher that she became the prime mover of a statewide meeting to discuss different methods of communication.

It was the same with the Leadership Training Program in the Area of the Deaf at San Fernando Valley State College.[2] Thrown together with deaf candidates, the hearing members ceased to see them as remote apparitions of the mind but as real, live human beings. So strong was the urge to communicate and so vividly were the difficulties and limitations of speechreading made apparent to them that they usually lost no time learning manual communication. Most of them will admit that they completed their program with a greater appreciation and a realistic understanding of communication and other problems facing the deaf mainly because of close association with the deaf.

The question might be posed as to why at first there is a negative feeling about manual communication. Aside from the feeling many have that it poses a threat to speech and speechreading development, perhaps it is a psychological thing, enmeshed in human nature—the fear of the unknown and the unfamiliar. As long as you can force the other guy to play "your game" then you have the upper hand.

People are more secure and comfortable in their native tongue. It takes real effort and sacrifice for many hearing persons to crawl out of their shells and into the skins of those they are supposed to help. Many fear it is too difficult, too late to learn to talk with their hands and therefore feel inadequate. They see manual communication as a threat to their economic wellbeing so the deaf are made to meet them 100% of the way. By some subtle machination of the mind, they rationalize that the deaf will have to live in a world of the hearing, anyway. The fact that

---

2. Later California State University, Northridge.

there are some deaf individuals who, having followed the precepts of oralism as a way of life and succeeded, comforts them and makes them more determined not to allow such an alien thing as manual communication to intrude.

Where does it leave us, the deaf majority? Are we to be, both literally and figuratively, the silent majority?

I have been told again and again that more of us deaf must go out to parent meetings, vote, go to workshops and to other meetings concerned with the deaf and that in one way or another we must learn to speak out, to tell others our side of the story, to cease acting as faceless apparitions hovering in the background.

Many of those whose viewpoints are diametrically opposite to ours are really dedicated and sincere in their beliefs. If we can reach some of them and help broaden their thinking, if we can show them that this is no Mideast war, that learning manual communication is not as difficult as they imagined nor harmful to the acquisition of speech and speechreading skills, we would be giving the cause of improving education for our deaf people a great boost.

Surely, the best ideas of the oral schools and of the combined schools could be selected and made to work for the benefit of our deaf people.

Who Represents Whom

From time to time adult deaf leaders of state and national organizations are criticized for the type of thoughts and feelings they express. For example, the November–December 1971 issue of the *Jersey School News* carried a talk "Regarding Communication Methods in Educating the Deaf" given by Dr. Pauline Jensen before the Katzenbach Parents Organization.[3] At the conclusion of her remarks Dr. Jensen stated:

> I find it significant that the spokesmen for total communication can speak. The best argument for early oral communication is that these deaf people who can speak intelligibly have become the leaders of the deaf community. For them, speech made a difference.

Another example was published in the January 1972 issue of the *Volta Review*. It was a talk given by Mr. George Fellendorf at a California Association of Parents (CAP) convention held at Concord, California, November 6, 1971. Said Mr. Fellendorf in part:

> Many deaf adult leaders of national, state, and local organizations were born, reared and educated during a period when use of the hearing aid was not considered appropriate or necessary for those identified as deaf. Since a great majority of these deaf leaders are individuals whose hearing loss occurred at later than the fifth year, it is obvious that these individuals do not represent my prelingually deaf child nor the children of many of you in the audience. Our insights into the attitudes and experiences of prelingually deaf and hearing impaired adults is quite sparse. Our primary sources are those individuals whose hearing loss was incurred prior to the age of 4 or 5 years and who are sufficiently articulate to speak out or write for the benefit of parents of future generations of children with similar etiologies and age of onset. Many of these individuals can be found among the ranks of the Oral Deaf Adults Section (ODAS) of the Alexander Graham Bell Association of the Deaf.
>
> The emphasis on preschool education for hearing impaired children, on the maximum use of residual hearing (which we know that virtually all deaf children have), and on the encouragement of parents to

The Deaf American (May 1972)

3. The Marie Katzenbach School for the Deaf serves students in the state of New Jersey.

take a role in the auditory environment and learning of young hearing impaired children is something which has taken place within the last 10 years. Thus, the young deaf person today, in his 20's, who had the advantage of having his hearing loss detected before the age of 2; who was fitted with monaural, if not, binaural, hearing aids; who had training from an experienced teacher or therapist before the age of 3; and whose parents were aware of and dedicated to maximizing the use of residual hearing, is indeed a rare individual in our deaf society today. This is a fact of which we as parents of deaf children and young adults should be aware as we evaluate the statements, attitudes and performance of many of those who are guiding us from the leadership among the deaf and the ranks of deaf organizations.

Realizing it or not, Mr. Fellendorf in his above remarks was throwing verbal smokescreens in a masterful way. To the uninitiated, his statements cannot help but appear convincing.

First, if what Mr. Fellendorf has said occurred the last 10 years then his own daughter and the members of the ODAS are too old to have benefited from the conditions he described to be of recent origin.

What is Mr. Fellendorf saying that is really new?

The John Tracy Clinic and other preschool clinics throughout the country are not of recent vintage. Maximum utilization of hearing aids and parent involvement are old hat to them. Generations of us postlingualists have grown up and struggled through the oral method. The training of the majority of teachers was based on oral-auditory methods. Rare, indeed, was a manual communication class for hearing adults. Those of us who did not spend our lives in a little or non-communicating family environment were lucky.

In all probability it is true that the degree and quality of oral-auditory methods have improved and that there is a more widespread and intense utilization of hearing aids. However, is it true that since we postlingual deaf were not brought up utilizing a hearing aid we do not fully grasp its merits? Aside from the better speech and language base that we have, are we really different in our experiences, thoughts and feelings from the prelingual deaf and the auditory-oral oriented children now growing up? Does Mr. Fellendorf leave the implication that the new breed of students will not need to use manual communication, that they will be better adjusted and will more easily integrate into a world of the hearing?

Let us go a little deeper.

It is possible for some degree of communication to be in evidence when there are hundreds, if not thousands, of practice sessions and repetitive processes. Of course, the deaf child will benefit greatly when families become involved and it always helps when attempts are made to utilize residual hearing. It should be recognized, however, that speechreading presents a formidable barrier to effective communication for the simple reason that a great part of spoken speech is not visible on the lips. To say that hearing aids will overcome the gaps and help the deaf child catch what he misses on the lips is an unfair and harmful statement to make. It is harmful because too many deaf children might hear sounds but not understand connected speech. Too many will be mistakenly treated as if they were hard of hearing. It should be self-evident that when one has impaired hearing sound becomes muffled or distorted and is seldom meaningful.

What often results is that assumptions are made that the deaf child is participating in the communication process while in reality he might be superficially participating or pretending or guessing or not participating at all. An onlooker can easily be fooled into thinking that there is participation. What is not realized is that contents of a topic are kept on a simple level. Thus success is more apparent than real. One need only take into account the universal reading and language shortcomings of the deaf and the fact that too many of them are underemployed to realize that it will take a multiplicity of methods to alleviate a bad situation.

In every group there are a few who stand out and that is what Mr. Fellendorf meant when he mentioned the members of the ODAS. (He failed to mention that there were only about 250 members.) In their positions, this type of deaf people are the ones Mr. Fellendorf and Dr. Jensen will meet. In order to meet others who are not as successful, they will have to go out "into the streets."

And this is precisely what many of us postlingual deaf leaders have done in our roles as teachers, officers of local, state and national organizations, helpers in clubs and social and recreational activities. We do not stop with little deaf children and generalize from what is observed within a limited age span. We meet with grown, prelingual deaf people in our homes. We listen to their problems, help them write and interpret statements, letters or documents that they bring with them.

Too many prelingual deaf people cannot write and express themselves but they transmit their thoughts and feelings to us. We become their spokesmen. Our thinking evolves from the hard reality of what we see and experience and not from a cursory acquaintance with an elite segment of the deaf population.

What is forgotten is that many of us postlingual deaf are teachers in schools and programs for the deaf. We are in contact with "the new breed" of deaf children Mr. Fellendorf speaks about. Recently I attended a workshop in which five schools and programs for the deaf participated. Many of the students were wearing hearing aids, they had early detection, training, etc., but their plaintive cry was the same that has been "heard" for years: Our parents do not communicate much with us, siblings tell us what is going on, not our parents, I do not understand my teacher in my integrated classroom, I have been forced to wear a hearing aid for 13 years and I could not think because I was bothered too much by sound, and so on.

The mushrooming population of prelingual deaf brought with it a new set of problems more diverse and complex than before. Unlike their postlingual counterparts they do not have a speech and language base and everything has to be taught to them from scratch. Moreover, many of them have additional handicaps which range from visual, emotional to aphasia and other forms of neurological and brain damage. Within the categories of the profoundly deaf and the hard of hearing there are sub-classifications or variations. Some might have enough hearing in the speech threshold frequency range which combined with speechreading skills help them communicate adequately on a one-to-one basis with hearing people. Others gaze uncomprehendingly when a person yells "Fire! Fire!" with all the clarity his lips can muster. Also, the ability to learn, to assimilate and recall information varies from person to person.

Thus, it became apparent to many in the field, that even with all the conditions laid out by Mr. Fellendorf, the oral-auditory approach alone was downright unrealistic. This is one reason why a new national parents organization has come upon the scene—the International Association of Parents of the Deaf—which is committed to total communication.

What is really new in recent years is the use of total communication as early as the preschool years. Only a few years ago rare indeed was the preschool deaf child whose parents could communicate with him manually as well as orally. Even more rare was the use of manual communication in classes for preschool children.

Do the Fellendorfs and Jensens think that we postlingual deaf people do not want our deaf people to be able to speak? For decades we have felt that if manual communication was used early enough the minds of deaf children will be stimulated and they will be more aware of what is going on thus resulting in a large vocabulary for them to speechread and to express themselves. We had to wait a long time for research findings to back us up.

Like Mr. Fellendorf, I, too have a prelingual deaf daughter. My desire for her to speak is as intense, if not more, than his. I have arranged weekly audiological visits for her and, of course, she is being guided to the wearing of a hearing aid.

Our primary concern, however, has been to help our deaf daughter develop cognitive and perceptual skills. We want her to be a thinking human being, having something to say and to speechread. There is no room in this article to describe the way manual communication has been an indispensable ally in her mental, emotional and personality growth, in her ability, at the age of three, to speechread and speak many words in a natural way.

We postlingual deaf say that there is not one shred of evidence that the use of manual communication will hurt the acquisition of speech and speechreading skills. Again and again we urge that the minds of our deaf people be developed first and that all helpful methods of communication be utilized toward this end. We strongly disagree with those who say that manual communication and oral-auditory methods cannot coexist and we invite intense experiments and research to settle this argument.

Whether one became deaf at birth or at the age of five, one will experience more incidents and problems that are similar than dissimilar. We meet the same cold shoulder, doubts, prejudices when we seek employment or when we try to purchase automobile insurance from certain companies. We turn on the television set and can follow so little of the conversation that we watch sports programs most of the time. Many of us are lost in group gatherings even with the help of hearing aids.

The fact that we postlingual deaf adults can speak, to refer back to the statements made by Dr. Jensen in the first paragraph of this article, is not because of our oral training for we already could speak before we entered school. (This should be made clear to parents.) What has made the difference is the fact that we became heavy readers and learned to think and write almost by our own bootstraps.

The President's Corner

" . . . deaf children often grow up without an awareness that there are different types of deaf people . . ."

It is ironic, if not abhorrent, that we who have fought against discrimination should ourselves discriminate. Witness the way some of us reject non-ASL users and/or those who prefer the aural-oral methods of communication. Instead of being sensitive and considerate, have we, who have experienced rejection by impatient hearing people, frustration in employment, inaccessibility to community services, become hardened to our own kind who act differently?

In the belief that the NAD gains strength when it becomes unified in its efforts and accepts different types of deaf people and becomes sensitive to their needs, I held a meeting in my home with members of the Oral Deaf Adult Section (ODAS) of the Alexander Graham Bell Association, the nation's foremost exponent of the aural-oral philosophy. In attendance were ODAS members Bill Bernstein, Christine Kemp, Kristen Gonzalez, and Jim Marsters. Gerald Burstein and I represented NAD.

We did not act in an official capacity, nor did we make any official decisions; we acted as concerned individuals seeking a common ground to broaden the horizons of our deaf people. How? Several ways were proposed: invite a representative from each group to address the other group; establish panels for presentations at meetings and conventions and to hold small informal meetings at different homes.

Of particular interest was the concept of an all-day workshop with a panel of deaf people of different backgrounds and philosophies which would include audience participation. We wrestled with the logistics of such a workshop in terms of location, composition of panel, type of invited audience, the possible dates and topics, the needed rules or restrictions. It was decided that the logistics could be handled at the next informal meeting.

Of concern was the realization that deaf children often grow up without an awareness that there are different types of deaf people with different philosophies, life styles, communication skills or preferences.

Would not exposure to differing viewpoints help broaden the mind of deaf children? Can we find enough volunteers who would be willing to invest time and energy to plan presentations at school assemblies, to set up a variety of social interactions such as picnics, parties, and other group activities? This is a key question.

During the A. G. Bell convention in Chicago last June, there was a workshop with representatives from four national consumer/advocacy groups: NAD, ODAS, SHHH, and NFSD. Here, again, there was a determination to find ways and means to interact and to find consensus of agreement on issues.

In looking back, I can recall the many articles I wrote, the speeches I made in defense of sign language and Total Communication. Some of my viewpoints were extreme but they were in reaction to the extreme stance of those who believed in the oral-only philosophy. I can remember my rising anger, my sweaty hands when someone condemned sign language.

Times have changed. Although there are pockets of resistance to any reconciliation of extreme viewpoints on communication methods, there is, overall, an enlightened perspective on acceptance of individual differences. Of the four ODAS members who gathered at my home, only one could not sign at all, which would not have been true in the past.

The people who gathered in my home are warm, caring, delightful. It is sad that there are chasms separating us. My imagination leaps when I think of what the possibilities would be if we were all working together to make the world a better place for deaf people.

Chasms can be bridged. Although we differ in communication philosophies, we have much in common. We all want to see barrier free communication in our society; we all want accessibility, not only in television, but in other areas of our lives; we all want meaningful delivery of community services, equal education and employment opportunities. We all would fight against discrimination.

Who knows but the small gathering at my home might someday turn out to be a pioneering effort that has led to an era of good-will, mutual respect, an effective cooperative working relationship, and a single unified goal aimed at improving the lives of our deaf people.

The NAD Broadcaster (February 1989)

President's Corner

If you have felt a high degree of tension at a particular time—make it a time in a pressure cooker—then you have some idea of my position and those of the staff at NAD's Home Office as the countdown to the nationwide March 1st Demonstration inexorably moved nearer.

At first, everything seemed gung-ho. Instruction packets were out to key people in those states who made clear their intentions to demonstrate. Media packets were also sent out. Two members of the NAD staff were assigned full time to activities related to the Demonstration. Phones fell off the hook ringing, ringing, ringing. One room of Halex House resembled a War Room as state activities were monitored.

Funds came in on a steady pace until they reached close to $20,000. Parents of deaf children called or wrote to express their joy that at long last something was being done for the years of pent-up frustration. At long last, we were finally reacting and doing something on a unified and national level about the deterioration of educational services for the deaf children. The deterioration did not relate only to the dwindling enrollment at state residential schools but to the breakup of day school programs, small or large, on the misguided convictions of those who narrowly interpreted the mandates of PL 94–142 to mean education with the non-handicapped in local home schools. Even pre-school infant programs that formerly functioned five days a week were reduced to two days.

Then came the thunderbolt—the announcement that Dr. Bob Davila was one of the nominees to replace Madeleine Will as Assistant Secretary of Education for the Office of Special Education and Rehabilitation Services (OSERS). Little did we dream that one of us—bona fide deaf, grown up deaf, educated like most of us were in special programs for the deaf—would be considered for such a top level position. It was almost as earthshaking as the reality that we finally have the first deaf president of Gallaudet University in 124 years.

The NAD Broadcaster (March 1989)

What do we do now? March 1, 1989 was a crucial date because it marked the anniversary of the Gallaudet University Deaf President Now protest. Reports came in that if we went on with the Demonstration, it would hurt Davila's chances. It was crucial that our actions should not backfire on him. His nomination was tenuous at best because, no doubt, other disability groups with their larger numbers could easily perceive him as antagonistic to their goal of non-segregation, although not true at all, and would inundate the White House with letters and phone calls in opposition to his candidacy.

Different states were at different peaks of readiness for the Demonstration. Newsletters had gone out calling to arms, to ARMS. Hundreds of phone calls were made to marshal support and disseminate information as to time and place for each group to congregate. Picket signs were made and ready to go. The logistics of transportation were already worked out.

It was important that we present a strong united front in keeping with the prevalent mood of our people.

There were about three weeks left to countdown. If we were to postpone the Demonstration then a week later we learn the Davila decision was made, either good or bad news, then what? Do we regroup forces and start all over again? Easier said than done. It is hard enough to change horses in midstream—but twice?

Also there were a good number of people who saw the Davila situation in a different light. They felt strongly that the Demonstration and the Davila situation were separate issues. They felt the Demonstration would not merely be a protest but an enlightenment. The world will know that we were not against mainstreaming for those who can make it or want it and that we respect the wishes of other disability groups to be educated with the nonhandicapped. We would have made it clear that our goal was for qualifying statements that would address the unique needs of deaf children. As more specifically, the Demonstration would be a fresh call for qualified deaf and hard of hearing people in educational decision-making and monitoring processes.

Hoping against hope that a White House announcement would resolve the Davila situation and that we could go on as originally planned, I held off a vote by the NAD Board on whether to continue the Demonstration or postpone. As the day came closer, the pressure increased until

I was told that there was an article in the Washington Post criticizing the White House for being slow in filling important federal posts.

This was the trigger that galvanized me into a decision to ask the members of the Board to vote. The vote was 10 to 3 to postpone. Ten days before the March 1st date, an announcement was drafted and went out to all Task Force members, State Association officers, NAD Board members and others that the NAD Board had decided to postpone with the hope that the states would cooperate. It was also made clear that NAD would support those states who for one reason or another decided to go ahead with the Demonstration.

By the time this goes to print, we should know whether or not Davila has replaced Madeleine Will.[4]

---

4. He did. After serving, Davila became the president of the National Technical Institute of the Deaf and then the president of Gallaudet University.

The President's Corner

Upon retirement where does a deaf person decide to live? There are retirement centers such as Leisure World, Sun City, Lawrence Welk resorts and hundreds of others of the same kind scattered throughout our country. There are a host of activities—lectures, special trips, operetta or theatre excursions, card games, golf or tennis tournaments—that happily help enrich the lives of our senior citizens.

Unfortunately, so many of these activities rely on a world of sound. Interpreters are either rarely available or too costly or there is no time to get one when unplanned notions hit the organizers. Friendships with other hearing senior citizens could make a difference, especially if they have learned to sign, but the ones that are deep and abiding are the exception rather than the rule.

No matter what age, deaf people tend to gravitate to where there is a deaf community. Thus we see large populations of deaf people in cities rather than in towns, or in places where there is a residential school or a college for the deaf.

There is a reason why over 90% of deaf people intermarry. There is a reason deaf people have their own bowling, golf, softball, basketball, Chess tournaments; their own churches or temples. Or why they are engaged together in a wide variety of social activities. Even oral deaf people prefer to get together with other oral people (ODAS), and hard of hearing people with those of the same ilk (SHHH).[5] If the reason could be put in one word, it would be COMMUNICATION.

Facile communication. Communication without tension, without strain or guessing. Communication that allows one to relax, to be yourself and to share one's thoughts with kindred souls.

A model of what I am talking about appeared in evidence when I stayed with my good, long time school friends, Ira and Shirley Lerner, in Margate (not far from Ft. Lauderdale), Florida. A score of years ago,

---

The NAD Broadcaster (May 1989)

5. Self-Help for Hard of Hearing people, now known as Association of Late-Deafened Adults (ALDA).

David Davidowitz, a hard of hearing teacher at the school for the deaf in White Plains, New York, had a dream. He wanted to establish a colony of deaf retirees who would be able to lead active retired lives. He himself would interpret or there would be interpreters readily on hand—for lectures on the stock market, on the changing legal landscape, on the medical aspects of growing old, etc.

Mr. Davidowitz's dream was realized to some extent. There is now a large group of retired deaf people, most of them from New York, who have taken up residence, either in the same condo unit or within a few minutes drive from each other. Their condo units are mostly two bedroom or one bedroom and den, two bath with a sunroom, kitchen and large living/dining room, all attractively furnished. In fact, the works of art that line their walls and the tastefully decorated rooms are impressive and a source of pride.

This community of deaf people is supportive of each other. If one is unable to drive or shop, others will pitch in and help out. Fridays are shopping days at the supermarket—a short walking distance—and beauty parlors for the ladies. There are weekly card games, of a variety to satisfy most who wish to participate, at the nearby Jewish Community Center and at AMITY, a church sponsored organization, and at the Broward County Association of the Deaf club room. At these spots, fundraising socials are also held.

There is intense competition at shuffleboard tournaments and weekly golf outings. There is a community within a community when deaf people socialize in their own homes with those for whom they have a special kinship that goes back to the days when they were in New York. They are often at poolside in the warm afternoons. Indeed, the pace of activities is dizzying and one can hardly be lonely. It becomes, happily, a matter of choice—either stay home and do your thing or join the crowd.

The matter of choice is crucial. In the world at large, deaf retirees do not have much choice, hemmed in by the limits which the boundaries of communication imposes on them. Take the concept of Elderhostels. True, Gallaudet University sponsors such learning trips but they are limited and sparse compared to what is offered to those who can hear and have practically half of a telephone directory of choices. If you are interested in a week of Shakespeare, in an outing to Yellowstone Park, in a boat ride down the Rhine, in a musical festival, they have it—for those who can hear. In no way can interpreters be supplied, unless one is willing to pay double the cost.

This is something well meaning people, the decision makers (the road to hell is paved with good intentions) cannot grasp or understand. Man's inhumanity to man is clearly in evidence when there is a blind pursuit to place ALL deaf children with the nonhandicapped. For the parallels, in the limited boundaries of communication for both deaf children and deaf retirees, hold true.

Poems

Lady with Mandolin

(upon viewing a portrait)

Sweet and angelic face
Eyes that softly gaze
From canvas framed by love,
What music floated from your mandolin?
What stories did your fingers strum?
Did they waft over a lover held in thrall
By your beauty and your music?

Do I catch the semblance of a smile
From a corner of your mouth?
How many times did you beguile
Troubled hearts?
What mysteries lie within
Your time, how brief the spark?

Music's ecstasies shine from your face
While deep in me love's music stirs.

Damsel, no need to strum your mandolin
For your tones will remain unheard.
Our silence is our common bond.
The intensity of the illusion of song
Suffices—for music has its underlay
Where silence never goes away.

To Bernard Bragg

Out of the shadows
Out of childhood dreams
From Fanwood, from Gallaudet,
You emerged and thrived
Grew in scope and vision
Into a teacher and player
Into a world traveler
On the world's stage,
A generous giver of your time,
Attracting a widening circle of friends,
With warmth and generosity
Earmarking to others needed funds.
You mind ever curious since birth
Bereft and starving for the right words
Aside from the language of the hands.
You struggle for flow of words,
For sentences that sing,
That break through the silence
Impaled on the fence of thought
Bloomed when books shook your being
And verbal language came with sign
Each feeding the other, interlocked
In thought and imagining—
Oh hands magically weaving song
And a tapestry of far-off places.

Actor, pantomimist, teacher, author, poet
Each gave you fame
But none the same
As your concern for fellow beings
And although deaf from birth,

With deaf parents, deaf relatives
You climbed the pinnacle of language flow
And carefully tuned your mind to grow.

Yours every right for pride.
Surely the angels were your guide.

The Arid Desert

When will the arid desert of my mind
Begin to bloom. Will someone, some kind
Stranger loom out of the hills and cry
Out some words that will somehow pry
Something out of an earthbound soul
And reawaken a long sleeping role
Will it be in the middle of the night
When I am half asleep and not uptight
Or will my mind click in broad daylight?
There is a strong insistent echo
Urging I do something before I go
To be something, to have something to show
But will I get nowhere, my voice a cry
In the wilderness, my heart all dry?
All my life this dream, this dream I had—
A speck on earth—yet a single lad
Who did good in a world gone mad
Who did something before he went
Oh, before his restless soul was spent.

My Four Senses

The glint of a far-off star,
The glow in a grandchild's eyes,
The friendly smile on a stranger's face,
The speck of a boat afar from shore,
Buttery rays sneaking into a dark room,
An endless vineyard,
A jetplane floating high above,
A windblown skirt
Revealing a sensuous thigh—
These are what I see.

Grandkids at Newport Beach in 2005.

The palpable heat of summer,
Suddenly effaced by rain,
Cheeks chilled by wind and snow,
A friendly hand on my shoulder,
Bare feet on pebbles at a cool stream,
The sting of a ball hitting my glove,
The soft touch of my dear one's hand,
The rise and fall of her bosom
In a long sweet fond embrace,
These are what I feel.

The aroma of barbecued food,
The sweat of bodies deodorized,
The passing of odoriferous gas,
The pungent lure of perfume,
The sharp scent of forest pine,
The bloom of the water lily,
The waft of chimney smoke,
These are what I smell.

The tang of onion
And tomato in the mouth,
The cool lick of ice cream,
The satisfying host of sweet candies,
The sting of a jigger of whiskey,
The savor of aged wine,
The flavor of seasoned steak,
These are what I taste.

The sparrow's song,
Warning cries of danger,
Plants whistling in the wind,
Barbra Streisand singing,
Strangers talking to me,
Familiar voices on the phone,
The lover's anxious sighs,

The noise of children laughing,
These are what I cannot hear.

No brooding quietude for me
Nor unwarranted fears
Four senses have I
Glad am I and I
Do not cry
For the one not there.

I Searched

I was alone and lonely
I searched and could not find you
Among a crowd of anonymous faces
All was a blur then your hands moved
In meaningful language—in Sign
And, as a squirrel scampers over a swath of snow
With its tracks extending till I could see no more,
The silence was suddenly broken.
Then and only then I knew it was you.

Times Past

Carried on blankets of air
To times past. This nightmare
Held your ghostly face
Substantial once and loved
But now a stranger
Cold, unfeeling and aloof
Recurring in nightmares only.
And to think I gave you my time,
My energy, my hopes, my soul—
Ah, the profligacy of youth!

The Big "If"

If my auditory channels were alive
Who would I be, doing what, going where?
A soldier buried in Arlington?
A famed surgeon wielding a deft scalpel?
A rich lawyer vacationing at the Riviera?
A womanizer, a pimp, a gigolo?
A maestro plucking a Stradivarius?
A singer warbling some sweet melody?
A bum loitering in the sun?
Oh, two roads diverged in the wood
And I, I had no choice but here I am—alive
Full of fantasies colliding in a confluence of "ifs"
Singing canticles of joy, pain and lost love
With voice silenced but the light still there.

I Fill This Small Space

I fill this small space, this time
Who is to say yours is better
Than mine or mine yours
Intensity changes within the minute,
The hour or the day
And we are but a speck but a gleam
Whose brightness flickers—
Yours or mine—it does not matter
The end of the road is the same.

Black and White

Plunge deep, deep plunge the knife
Centuries of grief glisten on the blade.
Burst the floodgates in a gush of blood.
Excoriate the white victim of your rage
For all hatreds, trampled pride, excoriate!

Expiated?

Then flee into the fingers of the night.
Why do you stand and tremble?
Is it the eyes mirroring your own despair?

Break, O Break! Penetrate the wall
Between black and white—

You

Who have tasted watermelon rinds and the whip,
Spark by whatever strange tympany of the mind
A nova on the universal harpsichord

Editor's Choice Award, National Library of Poetry

Hard of Hearing

Her auditory canal is a torrential river
Frantically seeking the anvil for the cochlear
When numb passages wounded by hairless nerves
Carry but some of the breezes waft with sound
Described then is she as hard of hearing.

The Cave Man

It was simpler in Paleolithic times
When words were unspoken or few—
A squint of the eyes,
A thumping of the chest, a wave of the hand
And Java man, in animal dress
Would go seek meat and try out roots,
No need to read lips
His quiescent unease and strange
But unmistakable gestures were fraught
With meaning, a grimace once or twice
And you knew it had to do
With life or death
Not the rigmarole of inanities.

To Err Is Human

To the nadir
Of an agonized soul
Pour down the anodyne
That will make it whole

Proserpine
At least was half awake
While I am clipt
By the cancerous foe

Since the incarnate snake
Spits sinuous woe
To the Pandora box
Of human hearts

I know only death
Reprieves
The thousand smarts
Of serpentenized Eves
So
Evil is human

First place—American Association of University Women Poetry Contest, 1948

Untitled — 1948

The torn fragments of my love
On the table lie
Gone forever the
Innate depth
The passionate sigh
That used to belong to me
Was my own shadow.
Now I gather the torn notes
Look out the window
And the infinite sky
Perceiving so clear
How yonder blue and she
Far away appear

Part Five

ON THE LIGHT SIDE – HUMOROUS APPROACHES TO DEAF EDUCATION AND EXPERIENCE

In these humorous pieces, a number of common themes can be witnessed: an optimistic outlook on the future of the deaf community, the invisibility of deafness, the humor inherent in being deaf, and an admission that Newman wouldn't mind if he could hear.

Newman's sense of humor was essential to being a teacher. He fondly recalls humorous moments in the classroom: "If students were off in their own world, I'd jump up and down to get their attention. And visitors would always be sure to walk by the door at that moment . . .

Reality Is Sometimes
Funnier than Fiction

A student was slouching in his chair. I decided to imitate him and demonstrated it—but fell off the chair . . . I gave test results and then a box of Kleenex to a girl who would always cry at her bad grades . . . During the Pledge of Allegiance, one of my students would mouth 'our father who art in heaven . . .' . . . one day the classroom was laughing at me. I asked one of the students, and he quietly fingerspelled: your fly is open . . . I went home and went to the mirror to check how bad it was, and how much of the zipper my jacket covered." Newman also remembers the antics that he and the NAD Board engaged in—late-night pranks, one-upping each other, and martinis in hotel lobbies.

I often have strange dreams. I once dreamed I was in the jury box while a man was on trial for his life. Every time the lawyer came near and looked at me piercingly, at least he seemed to, my heart thumped although I was in the second row behind a fat lady. I rushed through my mental file for what expression to use on such an occasion as this but could not twist my face to suit the situation. I decided in panic to take on a stony, mysterious, implacable, non-committal expression. It seemed to be working so I narrowed my eyes as a tour de force. The trial was over and we were locked up in a room debating God knows what. The discussions seemed intense, close. Everyone kept looking at me sensing that I held the key. I thought to myself that I would be silent for a while then I would spring the correct phrase, the statement of unshakeable logic. Suddenly all eyes were on me. Now was the time to make my move. I stood up slowly and slowly the words came out: "I am deaf." Everyone was electrified. Bedlam ensured, doors opened and flash-bulbs exploded. Mercifully, my bedroom alternated between light and dark as my flashing alarm clock brought me back to reality.[1]

The Deaf American (January 1969)

1. The provision of sign language interpreters was very different in 1969. Unlike then, today city and courtrooms are required to provide sign language interpreters for deaf individuals sitting on a jury.

Reality is sometimes stranger or funnier than fiction or dreams for a deaf person who tries to make sense out of a moving hole framed by teeth and lips. I do not know why but many times when I take a walk an automobile would stop with the driver obviously asking me for directions. Quincy Street is difficult to lipread and Brockton and Pocton are too close to distinguish so I would wave my hand majestically: "Three blocks down, turn left then after the first traffic light turn left again," never really knowing where they wanted to go. To this day I have a funny feeling that all the cars foolish enough to have stopped and asked me for directions are still going around and around looking for their destinations.

Now take the matter of change. Every time I go shopping I would give the clerk a $1 bill if I calculated the cost was 73¢ or a $5 bill if I felt the cost was below that and so on because numbers are exceedingly difficult to lipread. Invariably at the end of my shopping tour my pockets would bulge with coins or my wallet an abundance of dollar bills. I always knew immediately that the currency denomination was not large enough by the way the clerk looked at me or by the fact that the action of face and hands communicate more meaningfully to me than lips. In spite of the precautions I take the best laid plans still can go awry. Take the time I decided to be magnanimous and invite a couple to join my wife and myself to a Harlem Globetrotter basketball game. I gave the lady a $20 bill calculating the cost to be around $8 and waited for my change. None came. She looked up at me and sweetly said "Thank you." I looked up in search of a sign but there was no announcement of price just the statement that this was a charity game. That happened 20 years ago when the dollar still could keep its head up but I did not argue with the lady because in me there are traces of Caspar Milquetoast. I retreated with as much dignity as I could.

Sometimes I have this Milquetoast hangup bad. At a movie theatre when everybody laughs at something funny said on the screen I join them by shaking my shoulders. I have that disquieting notion that if I didn't my body would be scorched by all the stares. "What a humorless man" they would be saying.

My son pointed out to me what I suspected for a long time. "Why is it, dad," he said "people always come and talk to you when we go shopping?" Even if there were 50, 500, or 5000 persons surrounding me someone would invariably single me out for a chat. "Perhaps I appear fatherly" I told my son as I pointed to my bald pate. "Or perhaps the angels in heaven want to have some fun . . ."

The angels must have laughed uproariously that time when I was standing in line to the cashier with a bundle full of odds and ends and the man behind me began to talk. By some primitive instinct, I turned around and caught his mouth moving obviously in my direction. I did not know when he had started but instantly my face took on that artful expression most of us deaf are adept at when it comes to nodding, acknowledging, and sympathizing. The man kept on talking. I gyrated from one expression to another hoping I would hit on the one that would complement his supercharged mouthings. The man's face became persuasive, changed to quizzical and then was masked with a hurt expression. I noticed that my son, who sometimes mercifully interprets, had scooted out of the line and was gone. After a while the man's face grew redder and his lips finally closed shut. In the car on the way home my son cheerfully told me that the man was asking you "Why don't you talk? Why don't you talk" and all the while you were nodding your head with a sickly smile.

My wife, who is sometimes hard of hearing, taught me how to say regular gas while we were at the gas station waiting for the attendant. The attendant came over and words spouted out of his mouth. "Reegoolar gas" I said. Funny, but the attendant kept on talking. "Reegooooolar" I repeated adding a few more o's hoping it would be helpful. Instead of going to the tank of my car the attendant was still standing, his lips moving a little slower but his face straining to retain a trace of patience. Finally he lifted his fingers and he gave me the signal for 5 or 10. Only then did it dawn on me he was asking how many gallons I wanted. The next time I went to a gas station I had no trouble. What else could a gas attendant be asking? It was not lipreading but conditioned reflex on my part.

Often I would guess correctly what the other person was saying by a process of elimination or reasoning or anticipation. But, alas, it does not always work. One time I hit one of the longest drives of my golfing career. There was a foursome behind us who were awaiting their turn. One of them said something as I turned around. Surely he was complimenting me on my beautiful shot. "Thank you," I said. A hearing man who was in my own foursome immediately told me that the man wanted to know if I had got out of the wrong side of the bed that morning. My neck grew hotter as I tried to synchronize my "thank you" with his "got out of bed" statement.

Stop being silly I told myself. Tell them you are deaf and get it over with. Well, there was this good-looking girl I was dancing with. We were dancing beautifully because I kept in tempo by watching the other dancers out of the corner of my eye. Then she began to talk. "I am deaf" I interjected immediately. Putting on my most optimistic expression I added: "But I can read lips." I wanted to add that is if your teeth are not in the way but did not dare. The girl looked at me as if suddenly my ears had become elongated and sprouted horns. There was panic in her eyes and we were stumbling all over the dance floor. Mercifully, the music stopped.

A Brave New World

It is the 21st century. What a strange world and what strange goings on! It is an age of 99.9% successful transplants of the heart, kidney, brain—almost every part of the human body except the hearing apparatus. It is the scarcity of donors, not the lack of medical skill, that is to blame. By the unavoidable interplay of genes, especially the sneaky recessive ones, an increasing number of persons were born deaf until now only a relatively few are left on earth who can hear.

The deaf no longer find themselves in the minority. The presidents of General Motors and of the United States of America are profoundly deaf. In fact, each is the offspring of five generations of deaf families. The sign language of the deaf is now the universal mode of communication. Everyone feels sorry for the remaining hearing persons. These people as adults tend to form their own subculture with their own social and athletic groups brought about by their basic communication problems.

The hearing people have been allowed double tax exemptions and the United States government has taken pains to establish two colleges for them. Captioned films have been made for them after it was discovered that they were more effective than those dubbed with sound because it was difficult to synchronize sound with flying fingers and kaleidoscopical facial emotions.

Some hearing people who have acquired exceptional skill in both the receptive and expressive forms of manual communication have formed a group called the Manual Hearing Adult Society of the Abbé Sicard Association (MHAS). To become a member of this group one must use the manual method as a way of life. With evangelical zeal, many members of this group have taken it upon themselves to speak before parents of hearing children and teenage hearing students on the virtues of manual communication in a deaf world. The grace, smoothness and clarity of their manual delivery, the burning fervor of their eyes have left many witnesses visibly moved and impressed. The members of MHAS

The Deaf American (November 1969)

have been influential out of proportion to their numbers. They have managed to have their leaders placed on a national advisory board of the hearing and on other socio-political national groups. Sometimes they go too far and mail petitions of complaint to television networks that dared show persons speaking orally in one or two unique shows. When the National Theatre of the Hearing came into existence the editor of the *Abbe de l'Epée Review*, the organ of the Juan Pablo Bonet Association, sent telegrams of protest to the proper authorities complaining that the aforementioned theatre will destroy years of effort to inculcate good habits of manual communication among hearing students. A blasphemous article in *The New Democracy*, "Little Hearing Children," was ceremoniously burned and its author, John Edgeway, hung in effigy. Unfortunately, this tapped deep-rooted sadistic autocratic impulses among some of the more ardent MHAS members and several hearing aid users who passed by had their earmolds hammered into their heads. One victim survived, which the executive secretary of MHAS proudly stated reflected the compassion and dedication of the membership.

One cannot help but be sympathetic to the rank and file of hearing orals—oops—to the rank and file of the hearing. (The deaf public should be here warned that the epithet "orals" is an insult—it gives the impression that all of the hearing cannot talk with their hands.) The problems of the hearing are legion and typical of a minority group. For example, they are unable to understand shop owners, clerks or people on the street who communicate to them manually. It is of little or no satisfaction to them to be able to understand a few symbols such as the ones for "okay," "eat," "sleep." They feel ignored and frustrated at gatherings where everyone is talking manually and only a few—when the occasion or mood suits them—bother to translate, let alone, to interpret. Job opportunities and promotions are difficult to come by for some hearing breadwinners because of backward communication skills due to gnarled or thumby fingers, a missing finger or two, a stump where a hand should be, poor spatial receptiveness and weak recall which cause them to confuse one hand sign for another.

There is an Abbe Sicard clinic for preschool hearing children. This school admonishes parents never to communicate with their voices or to encourage their children to sue anything but manual communication because, it cannot be emphasized often enough, we live in a deaf world. Parents must attend this clinic in order to learn how to carry on the training at home. No interpreters are arranged for the many hearing parents of the hearing preschoolers so the clinic is dying on the vine because of dwindling enrollment. However, a new school, "The Manual Digital Institute," has been founded.

The hearing people have banded together and established a National Association of the Hearing (NAH) to fight job discrimination, to place their representatives on the government's staff in the Bureau of the Handicapped, and to protect their right to drive automobiles. State schools for the hearing have been established and although the superintendents and principals are deaf, at least 10% to 15% of the staff of such schools are composed of hearing persons who either teach retarded children or are on the custodial maintenance service. There are even Junior National Associations of the Hearing. The latter organization as well as the NAH and other clubs and organizations for the hearing are typically directed by hearing persons themselves such as Nivrem Nosterrag or Knarf Krut who are postmanually hearing, that is, they became hearing via rare auditory transplants after they had well established manual communication skills.

Many of the hearing have been able to excel in some occupations such as teachers of the hearing, computer programmers, employees in the graphic arts and the aircraft industry. There are even two full-fledged hearing dentists and one lawyer.

In the meantime, the deaf are now in the mainstream of society. They have had no difficulty becoming bankers, executives, ophthalmologists, shop owners. Some have undertaken welfare work to help those hearing persons who have remained on the fringes of society, who have become peddlers, and who simply have been unable to adjust to the realities of the world at large.

On Mini- and Midi-skirts

I think it was Thoreau who said long ago that if one monkey in Paris decides upon something everybody else blindly plays follow the leader. According to newspaper accounts there is now a "bouquet of beautiful women making a stand against lengthening hems and the demise of the miniskirt." These women have decided to stop following, like sheep, the whims of some fashion designer or couturier.

Calling themselves POOFF—Preservation of Our Femininity and Finances—the girls are led by actress Julie Redding and Grace Robbins, wife of author Harold Robbins, and their burgeoning membership includes Connie Stevens, Jill St. John, Liza Minnelli and scores of others.

"We love the miniskirt," Mrs. Robbins said. "Now we are all in trouble thanks to the fashion industry. Gradually they've been promoting the midi-skirt—about half-way down the calf. It's an unflattering line and we're going to fight it."

What brought about the drive for a lower hemline is subject to debate.

One school of thought holds that it is manipulation of consumers through planned obsolescence. What is good for the auto industry is also good for the fashion business. Let the cash registers ring louder throughout the land!

Another school of thought simply places all blame on President Nixon. To quote the newspaper account which quoted University of Wisconsin Professor William L. O'Neill, "We seem to be recreating the 1950s. Nixon is back in power, radicals are once again in jail and a recession seems to be in the making."

Indeed, there is the theory that hemlines rise and fall with the stock market and the way it is going I wish all women would hurry up and purchase only short skirts and dresses or shorten them. I wish they would hurry up and burn their midis and join POOFF.

The ladies of POOFF did more than joust sound off. In March they already declared POOFF week and they set up booths at various locations

The Deaf American (July–August 1970)

in and around Beverly Hills—chic department stores, boutiques, restaurants and hotels.

Deaf organizations could learn a lot from the ladies of POOFF. Mrs. Robbins, a striking brunette, said in the newspaper account, "We will have men and women by the thousands—maybe hundreds of thousands—sign petitions boycotting the new midi-skirt. Then we'll take the petitions to meetings with designers, buyers and mangers of department stores to discuss the problem. The girls will appear on as many talk shows as possible pleading their cause."

Mrs. Robbins went on to say, "We need help from women all over the United States, and we need their names and petitions right now, before Paris can dictate to us." She requested that females across the country sign petitions supporting POOFF and mail them to Post Office Box 1806, Beverly Hills, California. "Men ought to circulate petitions against the midi, too," she concluded. "They're the ones who will have to pay for new fashions."

For us deaf males, more than just money is involved. The midi-skirt is a threat to our happiness, well-being and mental health.

Shapely legs speak an eloquent language of their own. No subtitles are needed here. And when the wind blows and lovely thighs come into our line of sight our day is made. Exercised and refreshed, we are ready to tackle the other, more mundane aspects of visual communication.

Several questions, then, before us are: shall we continue to be the Silent Minority? Shall we remain aloof from such a vital sociological battle as the current mini- versus midi-skirt? Shall we continue to allow the public to carry on so many misconceptions about us such as are embodied in queries like: Can the deaf drive? Do they use Braille? One doctoral candidate wrote to the late Robert Greenmun asking if the deaf could swim. Bob's rejoinder is a classic: "I suppose that in order to swim people paddle with their ears."

And now our seeming apathy in the face of the titanic struggle to save our pocketbook, to show what the poet meant when he intoned "A thing of beauty is a joy forever."

Let us show the public we are a virile lot, vitally concerned in current events.

Deaf kneewatchers of the world, arise!

My Hernia Operation

The last time I had major surgery was more than 40 years ago. Now, in his office, the doctor told me to cough as he examined me. I obeyed instantly and coughed right into his face. This automatic response is a bad habit of mine. Psychiatrists might be able to trace this type of behavior to the tell-and-do activities of my childhood. You know—the teacher says, "Go, close the door," and if I can speechread that and respond immediately, I get a star or a piece of candy.

"You need surgery for hernia," the doctor said. His lips were the type you can sometimes read and sometimes not at all depending on the words used and the way he decided to move them. The fact he had a deaf niece made him a little more understanding. Then he said something unlipreadable. After two (2) repetitions he kindly wrote down what he was trying to say: "Are you allergic to any medicines?" It could be a matter of life or death, yet how many deaf persons could understand this statement, let alone speechread it?

"You'll now go to the admitting room," the nurse said to me. If I had a limited vocabulary or if my intuitive or reasoning powers were not there in the first place, I would not have detected on the lips nor understood the words "admitting room."

Before entering the hospital, I had made up my mind to quit nodding my head in a pretension of understanding. I WAS DETERMINED TO LET MY DEAFNESS SHOW. I decided I would not be like my wife when she was laid up in the hospital because of a miscarriage. The nurse said something to her. She thought it was safer to shake her head in a negative direction. Puzzled, the nurse said, "Are you sure?" For the next 20 years my wife kept kicking herself mentally because everyone but she was given a cool dish of ice cream. If there was anything she wanted most at that time, it was a cool dish of ice cream.

Simultaneously, I undressed, eyed the two-bed room, and the patient on the other bed. I noticed a *Playboy* magazine lying near him and made

The Deaf American (June 1971)

a mental note to ask, after my operation, if I could borrow it. The patient on the other bed had a friendly face, the kind that encourages a deaf person to take the initiative and strike up a conversation.

I was dozing off when abruptly I was awakened by a student nurse who tapped me sharply on the shoulder. "Roll over" were the words that could be clearly seen on her lips. My mind recognized the words but my body did not know how to react due to my soporific state. After a false start, body and mind synchronized and I rolled over and found myself on another bed. This one had wheels on it and was to transport me to the operating room.

The student nurse strapped me onto the bed on wheels and gave me a shot of something—I mean the needle type. I remembered a deaf friend of mine, who had a hernia operation several years ago, telling me I'd get a shot which would put me to sleep before I ever reached the operating room. I waited for blackness to descend and closed my eyes to help it on. Nothing happened—only a feeling of euphoria. I began to sweat a little. What if they started to cut me up while I was not fully unconscious? Instead of pushing the panic button, I decided to ask the other patient, who was now standing up, what the shot was for. Lips moved, teeth ground and words poured out.

"I am deaf," I said. "Please talk slowly and please move away from the sun." I talked with some apprehension, hoping to God I would be able to follow him. Fortunately, I was able to catch the words: "It is to relax you." He went on to say that the patient who preceded me had hernia, too, double hernia. He had a heart condition so had to be administered local anesthesia. The patient kept on talking but no other words were recognizable. Then the student nurse reappeared and chatted with the other patient, thoughtfully looking my way from time to time so that I could speechread her. She pointed at the *Playboy* magazine and chatted and laughed. I wished I could understand what they were talking about because I felt it would have been educational.

The student nurse picked up the *Playboy*, spread out the centerfold and flashed it in my face. Not wanting to appear out of place with the temper of the times, I shook my right hand to indicate "Wowie."

In the operating room one of the nurses had a face mask half dangling away from her mouth. Obviously she was talking to me. I sat on my elbows and pulled her face mask further down. The words, "What's your name?" came into the periphery of my vision. This was the fourth time they checked. It would not do to operate on the gall bladder of what was supposed to be a hernia patient.

Again, the nurse was talking to me but this time she remembered to pull her face mask down herself. "Close your eyes," she said.

The next thing I knew I was in the recovery room and then was wheeled back to the two-bed room. I noticed the other patient was no longer there and gone with him was Playboy magazine.

A new patient moved in. He was about 18 years old and must have been either in a slugfest or an automobile accident. He had a surly look and his eyes were always avoiding mine.

My pulse, temperature, blood pressure were checked every four hours. The next day a nurse, the "registered" brand, came in. "I'm going to wash your back," she said. She was a stunning redhead and worth two hernia operations. In a few moments she said, "Do you think you can wash your front yourself?" I could have said, "What did you say?" several times until she might have given up in exasperation and done the job herself. Instead, I chickened out and said, "Yes."

Before dismissing me from the hospital, the doctor gave me instructions for post-operative care. I noticed down the years that human beings like to do things the easy, short and simple way. People do not like to write things down unless they have to.

"Do not get what," I asked the doctor. After several spoken repetitions, he wrote down the word "fatigued." I could never have recognized it on the lips.

I have always thanked my lucky stars I have been a heavy reader. My education was what made me feel like a civilized human being. Speechreading is helpful in spots but an education . . .

It was good to be back home even if I walked funny. Before retiring at night, my wife asked if I would like a cool dish of ice cream. She has a habit of asking this.

Come to think of it, it is a persistent habit of hers.

An Encounter Group

This article was adapted from a newspaper article describing a weekend at the East Coast Cresalen Institute.

You never would have known it by looking at him. At Joe I mean. He stood there with his dark good looks and husky frame. His eyes are what gave him away. Brooding eyes. When not brooding they would dart in all directions like that bird—Iforgotitsname—which I saw at the zoo.

Many statements made down the years kept recurring in Joe's mind—"Never admit you are deaf . . . never talk with your hands . . . never . . ." Like an old refrain this statement kept coming back again and again: "This is a hearing world and . . ."

Deaf Joe, a grown man, was full of anxieties, his nerves stretched taut like circus wires. Unable to accept the fact that he was deaf, he avoided those who were deaf also and tried to align himself with those who could hear. Society's ills rubbed off on him—rich foods, alcoholism, and voyeurism as well as jangled nerves.

That was when deaf Joe decided to attend Cresalen Institute, a non-profit organization specializing in group encounter sessions whose stated purpose of "to explore those trends in the behavioral science, religion and philosophy which emphasize the potentialities and values of human existence."

Cresalen believes that through seminars and group sensitivity and encounter sessions one can be conditioned to use not only his sight but his senses of taste, smell, touch and hearing (never mind this one, Joe said to himself), to probe deeply into himself and develop a new consciousness.

Freeing the spirit, the mind, the body—a kind of joy and sensual pleasure in living and understanding the world—is at the base of Cresalen philosophy. A lofty and worthwhile goal, will it work for deaf Joe?

The Deaf American (September 1971)

Deaf Joe began the encounter sessions by sprawling on the green rug with 1000 other bodies of every age and shape and size.

"Rise and bounce lightly on your toes, eyes closed," the leader smilingly said but his beard practically covered his mouth and deaf Joe could follow only by watching what others adjacent to him were doing.

"Hands over your heads. Growl." Deaf Joe's hands copied everyone else's motions but he could not figure out what looked like banshee movements of the mouth. He shaped his mouth to look reasonably close to that of the other sea of mouths but he made no sound. He was afraid he would break the rhythm of whatever they were saying, be off key or out of tune.

Deaf Joe had no trouble following the next instructions. "Now laugh loud and long. Get inside yourself. Vibrate slowly, first your legs, then your arms, then everything. Breathe deep." Now everyone was getting into it.

Everyone was following instructions like automatons. They walked slowly around the room, looking intently at each face passing by.

Everyone was fleetingly touching fingertips regardless of sex and deaf Joe followed the motions faithfully. Then people were shaking hands while walking. Following instructions, passed on to him secondhand, deaf Joe lightly smacked every rear end he passed. He always wanted to know how it would feel to smack the rear end of a hearie. The pace slows and deaf Joe grasps both hands of the person next to him. He caresses her hands, then touches fingers lightly to her face and hair. Then he embraces her and moves on to someone else.

It was incredible the magic he felt reaching out and touching the fingers of a total hearing stranger. To him it was infinitely more sensual than the deep embrace. Could it be that thrust into a hearing world and striving to be like those who could hear, deaf Joe had felt more acutely the aloofness of those who surrounded him? And now he had just touched this pretty, dark-haired girl, this hearie.

"How do you feel? Make a sound like you feel," the leader directs.

Deaf Joe witnessed hundreds of different ways people were expressing themselves. In his exultation he beat his chest like Tarzan and like what he thought Tarzan must have done, he shouted: "Ahhhhheeeeeahhh." He looked to see if the dark-haired girl had heard him. Momentarily, he forgot the shackles that bound him. He wanted to go over to her and say "Me deafie, you hearie" but everyone was oblivious to what the other was doing.

People now lined up in groups of 20. They were told "If you feel like a leader, get to the front of the line. If you are a follower get to the back. You middle people fight it out for the center. If the guy in front of you doesn't belong there, get him out of your spot any way you can."

People were yelling and battling for position. Deaf Joe found himself pushed and shoved. Just like outside in the world of hearies he did not know what it was all about. A cheetah-like grin spread on his face. It was a way of releasing nervous tension. In no time, deaf Joe found himself in the back of the line.

Then the people were broken into groups of five. They sat in a circle, not speaking, sizing each other up. Here deaf Joe was in his element because there was plenty of nonverbal communication—touching, suspecting, emoting, hating, loving.

For 10 minutes they shook hands, held fingers and grasped shoulders. Once deaf Joe leaned over to touch dark-haired's face. She recoiled. Huddling tightly in a circle and holding hands, they were instructed to sing a song to the person on the right. Deaf Joe was serenaded by the person on his left with "Row, Row, Row Your Boat." Panic-stricken, he could not recall any songs for the person on his right. Profusions of sweat glistened on his face as deaf Joe tried hard to break the thick silence. Before he knew it, words came out of his mouth: "I pledge allegiance to the flag . . ."

It was all over. Relations at Cresalen were fleeting and illusory. The place depended for its success on the creation of a mood. The ephemeral nature of the encounter left its mark on deaf Joe as he walked out of the place. Outside people and cars were moving.

On the streets was reality.

Gestalt Learning

E very once in a while I receive a list of course offerings from the
University of California at Riverside. Usually, after a quick glance, I
toss it into the wastebasket. This time, I studied the list more carefully
because nine of us deaf teachers were trying to decide which course
offerings to select. We hit on "Gestalt Learning" perhaps because the
course title seemed chic and avant garde. It also seemed to carry with
it an air of mystery, of mind-stretching surprises to uplift our souls to
depth of insights and heights of teaching prowess undreamt of before.

It was a weekend course, three hours on Friday night, all day Saturday
and all day Sunday. If we survived the weekend we would be rewarded
with three hours of credit on a quarterly basis.

We were surprised to see the classroom, about one-third the size of
a football field, teeming with ambitious educators like ourselves. More
surprising was the lady in charge, Ms. Lederman. She seemed an older
version of the now generation with a worldly you-cannot-fool-me-look
on her face. I think she was bra-less. I said "think" because I had not yet
become acclimatized to my bifocals. She turned out to be the author
of a thin book (the title escapes me) whose unorthodox approach was
exerting an influence in educational circles.

Ms. Lederman half sat on a table in the middle of the front of the
classroom. Her eyes surveyed us. Her mouth did not open at all. We
stared at her. Silence. Nothing new for us but for the hearing people in
the room, the minutes must have seemed like hours.

We had brought with us an interpreter, Debbie Steele. Warm and lovable, she bubbles with enthusiasm, melts the hearts of men without, in
some mysterious way, evoking pangs of jealousy from the wives.

Debbie's hands stabbed the visual stillness of the room, indicating
that Ms. Lederman was finally speaking. "You do not need chairs," she
said. "Sit on the floor. Be comfortable." I looked around and noticed a

The Deaf American (June 1973)

goodly sprinkling of enrollees still on chairs. Girdles and aching bones can prevent full cooperation.

Ms. Lederman seemed to be measuring her words—no wasted words, just those that need saying. Debbie boldly stood besides her facing the classroom. When it comes to interpreting, Debbie has no inhibitions. She sparkles with the effervescence of champagne. Obviously, all those present, including Ms. Lederman, were captivated by her.

Suddenly, Ms. Lederman's words, as seen on Debbie's hands, hit us between the eyes. Know what she said? She said she wanted us to break up into small groups, each group to be led by a deaf person! Was she crazy or something? We asked Debbie to please repeat. We are not seeing things.

Then further instructions came. No one was to use his voice. We could communicate bodily or with our hands, arms, face, but voices, no.

I felt like an idiot as my group of hearing strangers gathered around me and eagerly looked at me as if expecting some miracle that will have us communicating with each other in no time. I started to make spasmodic arm and hand motions. Stalling for time, desperately hoping the molecules in my mind will whirl away the blankness, I started to wink my eyes and roll them ceilingward.

Somehow, without realizing it, I began to make myself understood. Decades of living with a communication problem helped. Man's primordial need to communicate brought to the surface untapped sources of creative ingenuity. We gave our instincts and other senses full play.

Smart cookie that I was, I introduced the manual alphabet. Soon we were telling each other how many children we had, where we lived, our exact occupation and that of our spouses.

On the second day, we were asked to go outside, close our eyes and move around like a blind person. Unsure, distrusting at first, I soon learned to relax in the hands and arms of the woman leading me in and out of light and shadow, around trees, up and down steps. Then our roles were reversed. Firmly, I wound my arm around her waist and led her around with my other hand.

We returned to the classroom, discussed our feelings of mutual insecurity that developed into trust. Warming up to the occasion, I told the lady to be frank and tell me how my voice sounded. "Too loud," she said.

I urged her to let me know whenever my voice passed the acceptable decibel range.

The third and final day we were to go outside and again undertake the role of a blind person, this time, we were to run. Full of trust, I ran. The lady fell behind. Suddenly, the thought occurred what if there were some obstacle ahead and she could not catch up to warn me.

When our roles were reversed, she ran with almost reckless abandon. Her resistance was gone and I let go. She was on her own. Her face shone with trust, with an air of full dependency on me. A cry from me and she would stop in her tracks waiting for me to catch up.

Back in the classroom, we assembled in one large group and again discussed our feelings. I found myself bravely talking to a large group of strangers when suddenly I felt a sharp kick on my foot. It was my "blind" companion signaling that I was talking too loud. The way the people were, the way we tried to communicate and understand each other, helped melt away some of my inhibitions. I went on talking, this time in a lower voice. Debbie said they were saying "Amen, Amen" to the feelings I experienced and which I vocalized.

The people in the room really were not strangers. You see people at a distance and barriers rise. The more you know them the less you think of them as white or black or oriental. Differences, even those of a physical nature, fade and the essential you emerges.

A letter from one of the students in the class sums up that memorable weekend:

Dear Debbie & Group

What a weekend we just had at UCR. The experiences I had will last a lifetime.

It is not often that we take the time to analyze our own fears and anxieties. However, this weekend for me was a time of tearing down and rebuilding. I was always anxious around deaf persons because I felt that I could not communicate with them. This weekend that anxiety was destroyed and in its place was developed an understanding and a love for the people in your group.

Why do we so often refuse to concern ourselves with things which seem different? There was so much to learn this weekend that I felt overwhelmed by my own ignorance. Yet, what I did learn was exciting and beautiful.

I will be coming (sic) down soon to visit you. But this is something I would like you to consider before then. If it is at all possible I would like for you to bring a group of your children to Big Bear for a day with my class. Consider it.

Thank you again for all that you taught me.

Rex R. Tift
Big Bear Middle School
Big Bear Lake, Calif.
P.O. Box 1111

P.S. What is Gestalt?

Yes! What is Gestalt? Does it mean to begin where the child is and take him someplace else? Does it mean not to teach, to move, to force learning until the child himself asks for help or is ready? I am not sure.

All I am sure is that we touched the lives of some strangers. We met each other half way and overcame some barriers of our own minds' making.

Oh, What a Beautiful Morning

I get up in the morning, look out the window at the rolling hills of the beckoning golf course, and begin to shave. I also begin to sing, splattering white foam on the mirror:

> Oh what a beautiful morning,
> Oh what a beautiful day,
> I've got a beautiful feeling
> Everything's going my way . . .

I have a dental appointment so I get into my car and no sooner do I park it when I look up into the eyes of a man in a pickup van. I get out of my car but notice the eyes of the man taking on a quizzical turn. I walk a few steps away wondering if the man is talking to me. By instinct, born of being deaf for over 40 years, I look around and sure enough the man is pointing his finger at my car. I had forgotten to take the keys and the motor was still running. This was not so bad. Not so bad compared to the time when I left it running until nearly a half tankful of gas was gone.

It was not so embarrassing as the time when I made a purchase and, after paying for it, left it on the counter. There were quite a few eyes staring at me as the clerk ran my way and tapped me on the shoulder. I tried to imagine what he was saying during the brief episode: "Mister, mister, you forgot your package. For Christ's sake, whatsammaterwithya?" And how many times have I forgotten to take the change, especially with the new dangfangled cash registers where change rushes down a shiny steel slide like bodies gliding down a curving slide into a swimming pool.

My eyes make every attempt to take over where my ears cannot. At the waiting room of the dentist's office a gorgeous lady was sitting nearby while I was attempting to read. I thought I noticed a movement on her part, and as quick as a six-shooter leaving its holster, I jerked my head in her direction. She was just scratching her nose. I have a bad habit

---

The Deaf American (October 1973)

of looking at people two or three times to see if they are talking to me. That I do it more often with those of the opposite sex who happen to be shapely is, believe me, purely coincidental and unintentional.

I felt relaxed in the dental chair because the hygienist had just the right shape of teeth and mouth for speechreading. I told her she should have been a teacher of the deaf. The dentist himself was the type I could speechread half of the time and the other half he would fill in with gesture or pantomime. He is much better than the barber who, at one time, when I told him I could not hear tried to talk to me by putting his mouth directly in my ear.

Now, I had to go shopping. Such a simple excursion can be an adventure. Usually, I am singled out by someone to talk to. A housewife would commiserate with me about the high cost of meat and I would nod lamely, not knowing the specifics of her complaint. A toothless little boy would say something and I would just smile. Watching him go to another person and following his movements I saw that it was the restroom he wanted.

At the checkout cashier line, the memory of the last time I was here flashed back. My son was with me and after we left the supermarket, he said the cashier was asking how you are and you did not even smile at all. I, a friendly and affectionate person, did not smile at all. This time I was ready. Before the total cost flashed on the register, sure enough he cashier opened her mouth. "I am fine." I said. Her eyebrows lifted ever so slightly and I could have sworn I detected the traces of a giggle. Her mouth opened again and this time the words came out "loud" and clear: "Anything else?"

You win some and lose some.

It was not as bad as what happened at the restaurant. Nine and a half times out of ten the waitress would ask "Anything else?" before presenting the check. And nine and a half times I would say "No." This time my hearing children were with me and all their faces became beet-red as automatically I said "No" before the waitress presented the check. "She was asking," one of my girls said, "if everything was fine."

Ordering from the menu is more troublesome. I ask for iced tea and get hot tea, for a cheese sandwich and get a more expensive chicken sandwich. I hate to make a scene so I usually try not to appear a bit flustered even if what I get is twice the price of what I ordered. At times I would gracefully allow my companion to do the ordering. Only trouble is he is deaf, too. But he is a smart cookie and does not open his mouth but, instead, points to what we want on the menu. We had a golf reservation for 7 A.M. and we had a half hour to go. All we wanted was pastry and coffee. Ten minutes passed then 15 minutes. Why should it take 15 minutes for pastry and coffee??? Twenty minutes. Twenty-one, twenty-two, then here comes the waitress with a steaming plate of French toast and sausages. My friend's bewildered look was killing me and I kept choking on my food. "Should we ask the waitress," I said, "when was the last time she was at an ophthalmologist?"

At the bank they have a new system. Formerly, I would line up behind what I thought would be the fastest moving line to the teller, but my luck was always such that I would be behind someone whose business transaction would be so complicated it took a half hour or more to finish. But now, with this new system everyone stands in one line and waits his turn for the first available teller. This is fine but usually there are 10 tellers ready to serve the customers and when I come to the end of the line I have to move my head in ping-pong fashion to see which one is available. Hearing people can just stand and relax until they hear someone call out that it is their turn. I have developed such good peripheral vision that many times I had to tell the hearing person ahead of me that the teller down to the left was waiting for her.

You win some and lose some.

I have a constant dread that my timing would be so good the bank would be robbed just when I am there. How do I speechread bank robbers who have their faces masked? How should I react—I am deaf, d-e-a-f, DEAF, don't shoooot. What do you wantmetodo? Lie on the floor? Turn around? Keep my hands up? In this case, I guess I will have to be fatalistic. Frightened by my "deaf voice" their guns will unhesitatingly go bang, bang.

Do not get me wrong. You learn to live with petty inconveniences. You learn to roll with the punches. How wonderful it is to be alive!

I arrive home. The golf course beckons. Calls from friends come in—how about a game of bridge, I know a place where we can dine, the captioned film for tonight is . . . . The television news program goes on and there are two minutes of news translated into sign language.

I look in the mirror. I notice specks of shaving cream at one corner. In my flat baritone I sing again:

> Oh what a bee-oo-ti-ful dayyyy
> Ev'errr-y-thinggg didn't go my wayyyy
> But I've a bee-oo-ti-ful feeeeling
> It could have beeen muuuuUCH worse . . .

President's Corner

"I became deaf at 5 years of age and thus belong to the rank of post-linguals."

The other day my secretary said to me "It is amazing how some deaf people manage to talk so well. All their lives they have never heard a single word." She went on to say "It is not just a question of voice quality but of pronunciation, of placement of the accent."

Indeed, I agree with her. I am not taking about those who became deaf late in life but of those who were born profoundly deaf. Some just had the talent, others developed their speech skills through the cooperative efforts of speech therapists, teachers, dedicated parents, and the early utilization of residual hearing.

It is a fact of life that two deaf persons may have similar audiograms yet their functioning level are worlds part. Both may have been born deaf, have the same education and training background yet one's speech is far superior to the other. This is one of the mysteries of life.

I like to take mental notes of various types of deaf speakers. They know that banquet is "bang'kwit" and bouquet is not "bou-kwit" but "bo-ka." They know you don't say "too pee" for "toupee." (It is tupa.) With impeccable ease they say "ker'nal" for colonel instead of "co-lo-nel."

I watch them speak with hearing strangers who will never know that the person they just talked with is stone deaf. If they knew, they would probably think nothing of it and assume it is the way it should be. I wanted to say "Hey, mister you have just witnessed amazing grace."

Place the same proficient speakers on a platform in an auditorium and the picture changes. At one time, there were one hearing and seven deaf speakers addressing a large crowd. Some of the deaf speakers had residual hearing, some were postlingual, having become deaf as late as eighteen years of age.

The NAD Broadcaster (March 1988)

In the audience was a class of sign language learners. They had little or no familiarity with "deaf speech" or deaf people. I asked them if they understood the speakers. They said they did not understand any of them except one—and that one happened to be hearing.

There is some explanation for this: ambient noise can be a detracting factor, or the microphone tends to distort one's speech, or the voice of the deaf speaker tends to trail off as the speech goes on.

At one presentation, an interpreter came to me and asked "why are you realistic and use a reverse interpreter while that guy doesn't?" I replied "Have you told him?" She said "No, it is too sensitive an area." I think it is up to us deaf speakers to double check and make sure the message is coming across.

I became deaf at 5 years of age and thus belong to the rank of post-linguals. I went to an oral school for a few years, took up speech lessons all the way to my late fifties. I was understood perfectly by my teachers, relatives, colleagues and those who have "deaf-attuned ears," that is, if you spoke in Yiddish they would still understand you. The older I became the farther away I seemed to drift from quality or understandable speech.

It came to the point where every syllable, every accent had to be said just right before I could be understood, especially by people who do not have deaf-attuned ears.

Yes, I am the one who said "too pee" for "toupee" at which time my brother interjected and said "to pee or not to pee, that is the question." I am the one who ordered beer for my thirsty companions when to our utter surprise we received glasses of milk. This has been a long-standing joke with my friends. Unseen by me, one of them was at the same restaurant where I was dining. He bribed the waitress to bring me a glass of milk after I ordered cocktails.

Indeed, using speech in the real world is for many of us an adventure in uncharted seas. My secretary, my children and others constantly admonish me to keep my voice down. Someone stated that when I am angry my voice sounds like a roaring waterfall. Recently, at a restaurant I thought I was asked if I wanted potato salad, cole slaw, or beans. I chose beans—and was given a glass of beer. Apparently, the "b" sound is clear but not the rest.

It is possible for a deaf person to think a word is pronounced a certain way for 10 or 20 years or more before being corrected by someone. For me, such was the case with "lingerie." For 40 years, I thought it was spoken somewhat like "link-er-ee" only to be corrected by my secretary (she's also my speech teacher). She told me it was "lan-ja-ra." I wonder if those aforementioned fabulous deaf speakers would have known it?

French and some Spanish words give me problems. I must remember that the "J" in my street name of Via San Jacinto is pronounced "Haci-nto." New terminology that is developed in keeping with current needs also give me problems. When I order "Nachos" I am not sure if it is pronounced with a hard or a soft "k." I was told how to pronounce it but I keep forgetting. I did order it at a baseball game—the wrong way but still got my nachos. The woman at the counter must have put two and two together and figured out what I wanted.

I always have problems with words that have an "x" in it, especially "exists," "exciting," and I have to store in my memory the fact that in "sit-uation" the first "t" is a soft "t" almost like an "s." I wish I had the com-puter memory with which my fabulous speaking deaf friends are blessed. When I say "superintendent," it drawls on to "superintentendentdent."

Oh well, I will just go to my favorite restaurant and order a glass of beans.

The Violins

There was this opulent exterior of a Mexican restaurant. Inside it was as classy looking as it appeared outside. As soon as we looked at the menu, we found the prices surprisingly to be reasonable. There were eight of us stone deaf adults seated around a heavy dark oak rectangular table. Of course, a circular table would have been preferred. This preference, I daresay, is one item of deaf culture since a round table brings everyone within eyesight and thus facilitates the communication process. But it would mean a half hour to one hour wait for this table and we were hungry.

No sooner was I seated then out of the corner of my eye I noticed a band of musicians moving from table to table. Most were playing on violins while one strummed a guitar. Do not ask me how "strummed" is supposed to sound or how I know when to use the word. I have read the way others have used it thus it seems the appropriate verb. Anyway, we have seen on television or at the movies how a romantic swain and his lady friend were at a table in a dark corner of a restaurant. On the table was a lone candle burning, setting off a mood of romantic ambience. As if foreordained with a generous gratuity, musicians came to this area. Music is said to have charms to sooth—And yes, the lady friend seemed all aglow and what resistance she had to the young swain must have melted as the notes of the violins wafted her to giddy romantic notions.

But to come back to reality, what are a bunch of us stone deaf adults supposed to do when the musicians come to our table? We have choices.

There are deaf people who don't give a damn, who have no reservations about how non-deaf people view them. They will just be themselves. They even consider themselves tough and often use the sign for "tough"—a clenched fist hitting the chest. The more passionate they feel about this the harder they hit the chest. (Warning: females learning to sign have to be careful to make sure the clenched fist hits above the breast area). Another method to express tough feelings is to use the expression "deaf power" by covering one of the ears with one hand and with a clenched fist of the other hand pummel the air.

Mervin Garretson, ed., *Perspectives on Deafness. A Deaf American Monograph* (1991)

And there are other deaf people who are sensitive, perhaps overly so, on how others view them. They do not want to be viewed as different. They would rather blend into the landscape of the hearing world. Perhaps, their childhood experiences tuned them to be this way. It could be their parents telling them not to sign, at least not in public. It could be other children staring at them causing acute and uncomfortable feelings of being different.

Anyway, sure enough the three violinists and the guitar man came to our table. They seemed so focused on their playing that they did not realize they might as well have played to an empty table. And what did the eight of us do? We were disparate in our upbringing, in our school experiences, in our attitude to the world around us. None of us could tell the difference between a guitar and a violin and would probably have considered Rachmaninoff's "C-Sharp Etudes" as something to do with C-section births.

At first, we carried on with an air of insouciance, then the irony of the situation hit us. Vainly, we tried to suppress a spasm of giggling, some of us covering our mouths with our hands. We were not the clenched-fist-beating-on-the-chest type nor were we the cringing overly-sensitive-to-what-others-think-of-us type. Perhaps, we were somewhere in-between, moving on the fringes from one extreme to another depending on the circumstances.

The musicians must have taken our actions as a show of little or no interest, still not realizing that their music took detours. They moved on to the next table. I was tempted to give the head player a tip to make perfect the irony or illusion but for some reason I did not do it.

This brings up the perception of music. Most of us probably do not think about it or have relegated it to somewhere in the subconscious. But I often wonder about it. What does it sound like? A singer singing with passion as can be judged by the tremors of her open mouth, an opera star who can go higher and higher without being asphyxiated, the background music as a movie film opens, a rock band going thump-a-thump ba-boom which most of us deaf people can feel but which is still different from hearing it.

Music is the number one interest of most hearing people. I try to understand it, try to imagine the transfixed state of the audience listening to a Frank Sinatra, the tingling sensation that runs up the arms and down the spine, the feel of your whole being entering an unearthly dimension. How does the "Lullaby" by Brahms sound? What about Tchaikovsky's immortal Piano Concerto No. 1?

Oh, tell me what carrying a tune means. What does the beat, the rhythm feel like when America sang "Mairzy Doats," or "Aba Daba Honeymoon" (sung by Debbie Reynolds and Carleton Carpenter)? What about Danny Kaye singing in his supposedly unique and funny way "Chickery Chick"?

There are many of us like my wife, Betty, who had enough hearing left to listen and be moved by music. Her favorite was the duet of Nelson Eddy and Jeanette McDonald. She would listen to them a thousand times until the time arrived when she had a vascular attack and all of the hearing she had left was irretrievably gone. It is a greater tragedy for those like her than for us who have never heard at all.

There are still many among us who have some hearing left, who tend to use headphones or their own hearing aids to listen to music.

I have asked them to describe the lilting tunes but they could not. Apparently, music is something to be heard and felt and is beyond description.

At this point, I thought of Edgar Allan Poe's stanza on the Angel Israel. The words ran something like the following:

> If I could dwell
> Where Israel hath dwelt
> And he where I
> He would not sing so wildly well
> A mortal melody
> And a sweeter note than this would swell
> From my lyre into the sky.

Which brings up the barbershop quartet of Norwood-Sullivan-Carney-Schreiber. They were an unforgettable sight pounding away with timely and popular songs. They must have been flat or toneless but who cared. At the slightest pretense they would quickly get together and let go.

Yes, Virginia, there are deaf people—not necessarily with much hearing left—who sing and play musical instruments. If it gives them pleasure, then more power to them.

As for me, every time I think of it a cold sweat rushes over me.

I must have been 11 years old at that time. It was at a birthday party for one of the kids at a summer resort in the Catskill Mountains in New York. Each child in turn around the large table stood up and belted out a song. Remember, I had no conception of what music is, let alone a song. When my turn came, apparently there was apprehension among the adults standing around. I stood up and went "EEEEEEEE AAAYYYYY IIIIIIIIIII-whooooo, lullallaallawah," not knowing what in hell I was doing. It must have gone on for several minutes and when I finished it looked like I got the most applause. Years later, I realized they were clapping in relief that I had stopped before their eardrums gave out.

The experiences of deaf people in the world of music must be as varied as the number of deaf people themselves, ranging from no involvement at all to finding a different outlet such as in poetry.

The violins at our table at that restaurant gave the illusory picture of normalcy but the term "normalcy" is relative. Couched in deafness 24 hours a day, for most of us music is not part of our normal routine.

The world goes round with the play of stringed instruments, the tooting of horns, the beating of drums, the arias in operettas, the mellifluous songs of nightclub singers.

And we, like the postman, rise up at dawn, give a shrug at what we do not hear and go to our appointed assignments.

Betty and Larry at a Gallaudet alumni reunion.